step-by-step / 001 /

digital landscape photography /

001

step-by-step / 001 /

digital landscape photography /

Tim Gartside

ILEX

First published in the United Kingdom in 2003 by

ILEX
The Old Candlemakers
West Street
Lewes
East Sussex BN7 2NZ
www.ilex-press.com

This book was conceived by

ILEX
Cambridge
England

Publisher: Alastair Campbell
Executive Publisher: Sophie Collins
Creative Director: Peter Bridgewater
Editorial Director: Steve Luck
Design Manager: Tony Seddon
Series Editor: Stuart Andrews
Editor: Ian Probert
Designer: Jane Lanaway
Development Art Director: Graham Davis
Technical Art Editor: Nicholas Rowland

British Library Cataloguing-in-Publication Data
A catalogue record for this book is available from
the British Library

ISBN 1-904705-13-8

Printed and bound in China

For more information on this title please visit:
www.sslauk.web-linked.com

Contents

Introduction

A telephoto lens was used to zoom in on London's St Paul's Cathedral and a tripod helped keep the image sharp over the eight-second exposure. The moon was added later.

The colours of this shot are not manipulated. Night scenes come alive with colour as all the different light sources blaze away. Tungsten creates a warm glow, while mercury vapour lights create an eerie green. Use these colours to your advantage rather than trying to correct and change them.

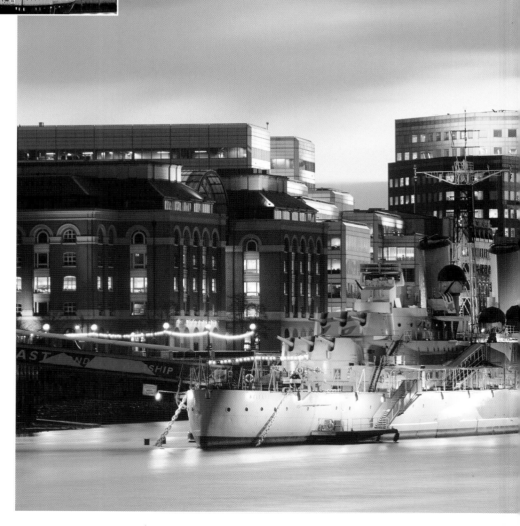

Taking a photograph is the end product of an emotional journey. Quite often, however, the final result is disappointing when compared to the memories of the original experience. Human vision is vastly superior to that of a camera lens and CCD. Along with visual memory, we also store emotional feelings about the moment – this is something that is a long way off with digital cameras! It is impossible to relay the full impact of the original moment because a print is two-dimensional, flat, without depth and emotion. We can, however, use the picture as a reminder, and the more powerful the image, the greater the stimulation we will feel. If you can learn to maximize the quality of your prints, then you can also maximize their emotional impact.

Bodiam Castle, Sussex, was shot at dusk and the image was brightened on the computer. The full moon was added to the picture later. The sky in the shot of the Alhambra, Spain was also brightened to enhance the dramatic effect.

Human vision is much wider than a camera lens. This is because we are able to easily move our head and eyes around to create a 360° panoramic image. This is also part of the reason why a print fails – it simply cannot recreate the full image that we remember. With the stitching together of multiple shots we can now come closer to the impact of the original scene. Perhaps one day a digital camera will produce a 360° image that can be projected onto a screen in a small room to truly relive the moment.

The invention of photography was supposed to usher in the demise of fine-art painting: centuries of customs wiped out overnight. Of course, this was the opinion of a small minority of doom-and-gloom merchants getting all upset about nothing. In fact, this new medium created a fresh and exciting avenue for artists to explore. The doom-and-gloom merchants are back, however, claiming that digital photography will destroy traditional film photography as we know it.

As with most new technologies, there is an initial resistance and reluctance to embrace and learn digital photography. We are a suspicious lot and on the whole most of us don't like change, as with it comes the need to learn new methods. It is an inevitable fact now that digital cameras and pro digital backs will replace analogue film cameras as the medium on which to capture images. How quickly this will happen is difficult to predict, but the big push will come when price and quality equal or improve upon traditional film cameras. I predict a niche market will always be there for film – especially black-and-white fine-art prints, which will become more sought after as prized pieces of photographic art in galleries.

Years ago, as a photographer in the reprographic business, I was fortunate enough to recognize the creative potential of digital image manipulation. It was, however, some time before I could afford to purchase my own computer system. In the early days, computer systems would cost hundreds of thousands of pounds and need several huge magnetic tapes on which to store the digital information required for one image. These systems were housed in huge air-conditioned rooms. Nowadays, however, a digital system is more affordable and the average hard drive can store many times the capacity that roomfuls of digital tapes used to hold. Technology increases and cost decreases – both are advantageous to us, the consumer.

As a stormy day drew to a close I was waiting for some fireworks in the colour of the sky. I was certainly not disappointed on this occasion. Stormy weather that clears in time can create some great skies for photography. The texture, shape and colour of these clouds add to the drama of the subject, especially when reflected in the river.

Using a zoom lens has allowed me to create and combine several interpretations of this river scene by varying the focal length and changing the composition over time. I shot the scene over a 30-minute period, shooting as the ambient daylight changed and a sunset glow faded into evening dusk.

Introduction

Introduction

 Capture the rich colours and splendour of autumn. Zoom in to emphasize one stunning tree and use a polarizer for intense colours.

These brilliant sunflowers were brightened up and the sky enhanced, to give a vibrant, colourful image. Careful selection of the sky with the Lasso tool was essential to maintain a realistic look.

INTRODUCTION

The upside of digital photography is that you don't need film – in theory you should save money in the long run. This will depend on the cost of the camera and all the peripherals required to create an image. Another major advantage of digital photography is that it is instantaneous – you can view within seconds what you've just shot. To do this traditionally requires Polaroid film, which is horrendously expensive. The main disadvantage of downloading large files onto a memory stick or mini hard drive is the cost of the memory, although it is constantly falling in price. Storage capacity is also getting better and smaller in size, which will be necessary as image files increase in size.

Power consumption is another problem that is being resolved as power supplies become smaller and last longer.

The chief hurdle to overcome is that to get the most out of your digital images you will need to learn how to manipulate them on a computer. The main advantage of using a computer is that you don't need a smelly darkroom or one-hour lab to do your image manipulation. You can do it in the comfort of your own home or, if you have a laptop, just about anywhere you fancy. The digital darkroom is clean, warm, comfortable, bright and you don't need to convert your bathroom into a darkroom any more!

Digital gives you more control over your images than ever before. You can produce prints that the best print labs would be proud of and even create prints that to produce traditionally would be very expensive or even impossible. In this book I shall be discussing all the traditional photographic techniques you

will need, such as cropping, colour correction, tonal adjustments, dodging and burning, as well as digital techniques such as using filters, sharpening and using layers to create montages. All the techniques you require to create a masterpiece that you can proudly hang on the wall.

Future digital image-makers will blend together photographic reality with painting and illustration in order to create a new art form that combines the best features of both worlds.

These flowers were taken from several different angles, all shot at the same location under the same lighting. This is important for a coherent and homogenous effect. A sunlit sunflower would stick out like a sore thumb.

1 Your digital camera

Once the poor relative of the film camera, the digital camera is rapidly approaching a point where it will match and even better its precursor. In fact, if the new technology has a weakness it's the frantic rate of obsolescence. Whatever camera you buy, it will only be a few months before a better model appears. This makes it crucial to know what you are buying before you splash out. Take a deep breath and get ready to jump into the digital world.

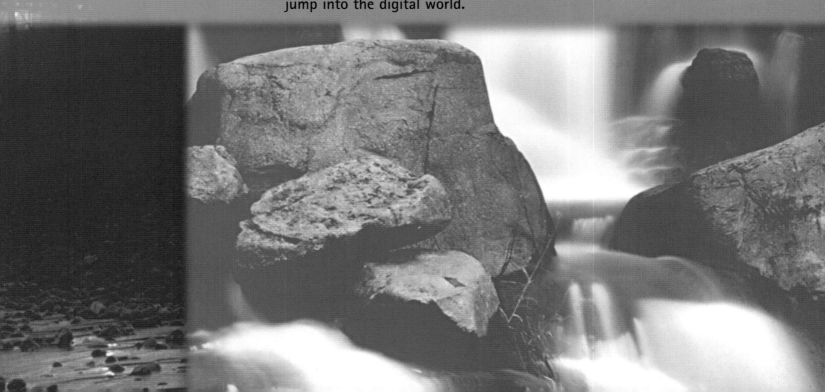

The camera and its controls

The rear of the Nikon Coolpix 5700, an excellent mid-range digital camera. Visible on the left are the viewfinder and, below, the swivelling LCD monitor. On the right you can see the buttons and control pad for navigating the menus, the flap covering the card slots, and the zoom control.

Before making the leap into the digital age, it is essential to have an understanding of the various components that make up a digital camera. This simple guide illustrates the differences between traditional and digital cameras.

CCD (CHARGE-COUPLED DEVICE)
These are usually two-thirds of an inch in size and are used in place of film to capture the image as it exposes. Each CCD is made up of tiny light-sensitive silicon photo diodes that capture the light as it shines on them.

LENS/DIGITAL ZOOM
Ignore the digital zoom ratio and look out for the optical resolution. The greater the optical zoom range, the better. Digital cameras do suffer from not having very wide-angle focal lengths. The widest is usually 7.0 to 8.0mm, which ranks as the equivalent of a 35mm wide-angle lens.

AUTO-FOCUS/AUTO-FOCUS MODES
Most cameras offer manual or auto-focus modes. More sophisticated models have five- area multi auto-focus. You can choose which area in the frame your subject will be in and the auto-focus will concentrate in that area.

From above the camera you can see the shutter release and the mode dial on top of the handgrip, the LCD panel, which displays useful information on exposure and shots remaining, and the accessory shoe, which allows connection to an external flash unit.

LCD MONITOR/VIEWFINDER
One of the most obvious benefits of shooting digitally rather is that you can see what you've just shot on a colour screen. Try to get a camera that also has a standard optical viewfinder.

STORAGE
Most cameras use Compact Flash or Smart Media cards, but you can also find Memory Stick, SD Memory Card, XD Memory Card and Microdrive. The last format offers the highest storage capacity of up to 4 Gigabytes. Other cards come in sizes from 16 to 512 Megabytes.

CAPTURE MODES
Most cameras have the option to shoot in several file formats. In most cases, the best is TIFF. Some higher-spec cameras offer a RAW file format, smaller in size than a Tiff but still retaining all the original data. The last option is usually a compressed JPEG format. JPEGs are smaller, so you can pack more onto a memory card, but there is always some loss in quality. Having said that, the highest quality setting still provides good results.

The range of digital cameras can be bewildering. A 4 megapixel camera with a good zoom range and manual controls would be a starting point. A high-end digital SLR is ideal if you have the funds available to afford it.

SHUTTER

While not all digital cameras have shutters, most have a control that simulates the effects of shutter speed in film photography. If you are interested in night shots and low-light photography then make sure that the camera is able to take long exposures. A shutter speed of 15-30 seconds is essential. Expensive cameras can shoot several frames per second, but for most landscape work that's irrelevant.

APERTURE

The aperture, also known as an iris or diaphragm, is a hole at the end of the lens that has up to seven blades to create the round shape needed. This and the shutter speed control the exposure and depth of field.

EXPOSURE CONTROL

More sophisticated cameras have several modes to choose from, including auto, programme, aperture priority, shutter priority, scenes and manual. Scene mode usually has several settings, such as landscape, portrait, night and so on are good starting points for a beginner.

EXPOSURE METERING

More sophisticated cameras offer a wider choice of modes to choose from. These include segment or matrix metering on most models.

EXPOSURE RANGE

The exposure value or EV range can be from -2.0 to +18.0, which would equate to using ISO 100, 200, 400 and 800 speed film. The ISO rating is an internationally recognized standard for the light sensitivity of film. The higher the ISO, the more sensitive the CCD.

SENSITIVITY

The sensitivity of a CCD is referred to as its dynamic range. The higher the figure, the better. Background noise has always been a problem with digital cameras, especially in low-light situations. When the CCD can't pick up enough information, it creates patterns of white pixels which show up in dark areas.

WHITE BALANCE

White balance is used to correct any colour casts present in the shot. Most cameras allow an auto white balance to be taken, and some cameras allow the white balance to be changed using preset modes.

FLASH

Most digital cameras come with a small built-in flash. For more serious work you need to buy a separate hand-held flashgun.

BATTERY

Digital cameras are battery-hungry. When using the LCD monitor and downloading to a storage card you use a lot of power. Rechargeable batteries offer the best route to economy.

IMAGE RESOLUTION/FILE SIZE

The image size and resolution of a picture directly relate to the size of the file you save to your memory card or the hard disk. Digital cameras come in a variety of resolutions : usually known as megapixel ratings. More expensive cameras have higher megapixel ratings: top-of-the-range models are now capable of capturing up to 15 million pixels, but the quality of even 3 megapixel cameras can be surprisingly good.

▶ A 3 megapixel camera uses a maximum pixel size of 2100 x 1500. At 72ppi it can produce a 29 x 21-inch print, but at the recommended printer resolution of 300ppi it will only produce a file size of 7 x 5 inches.

▶ A 5 megapixel camera can produce a print of 8.5 x 6.4 inches at 300ppi.

▶ A 6 megapixel camera can produce a print of 14 x 9.5 inches at 300ppi.

The front of the Nikon Coolpix 5700, showing the shutter release, the 8x optical zoom lens and the flash. The Coolpix 5700 uses a 5 megapixel CCD – to get better image quality you would need to go further up the price range to a digital SLR camera.

TIP Buy a camera with a good zoom range or an SLR with interchangeable lenses for maximum flexibility. Get the best you can afford. Skimping only leaves you disappointed and desperate to upgrade.

The lens

Choosing a lens suitable for the shots you plan to take is of paramount importance. The wide diversity of lenses available to photographers can be mind-boggling. Although some lenses have distinct advantages over others in certain situations, you will find that your digital camera's built-in lens is more than capable.

Lenses have two main controls – the aperture and the focus. The aperture is a diaphragm that opens and closes, allowing more or less light in. In conjunction with the shutter speed, this controls the exposure. The lens also rotates to focus from close-up to infinity.

Having the right lens for the right job is essential. Most digital cameras come with a fixed zoom lens, which will suffice. Choose a camera that has a good range from wide-angle to telephoto. Most fall down at the wide end of the zoom. If you are making the change from conventional-film SLR cameras you will find many digital cameras can't manage much more than 35mm or 28mm at most.

Most digital camera use a CCD sensor size smaller than the traditional 35mm camera film size, which effectively makes lenses about 1.5 times longer. A 28mm lens thus becomes a 42mm lens on a digital camera.

If you like your shots super-wide or super-long you may need to buy a pro SLR digital camera with interchangeable lenses. If you already own such exotic lenses this could be your best route. The latest 13 megapixel cameras have full-frame 35mm size CCDs.

WIDE-ANGLE LENSES 20MM–45MM

Even at 28mm such a lens would only just be considered wide-angle these days – 14–20mm is now the norm. With digital photography, however, it is possible to use a shorter focal length with success. Indeed, 'panoramic stitchers' exist that allow panoramic shots to be made by joining together several shots.

The other strength of wide-angles is depth of field (see page 17). Most shots will have foreground to background sharpness at f8 or more. Only when shooting a subject at closer range will smaller apertures be needed to maintain front-to-back sharpness.

Wide-angle lenses have a dynamic effect on landscapes. Sweeping vistas take on a feeling of fantastic depth because more can be taken in than the angle of natural vision.

These two shots show the maximum and minimum focal lengths of a zoom lens. Zoom lenses are very versatile as they allow you to precisely compose your shot before pressing the shutter button.

▶ These shots illustrate how zooming in on a subject can isolate detail within the wider shot. How far you can zoom in depends on your lens' focal range. Wide-angle and telephoto converters can be fitted to a lens to give it extra range. Try to buy a camera with the widest optical zoom range that you can afford.

STANDARD LENSES TO SHORT TELEPHOTO 50MM–135MM

A 45–50mm focal length is similar in angle of view to our own field of vision. It brings things a little closer, but without the severity of a telephoto. It is good practice to slow down the zooming process and look at the world at several stops on the way.

The short telephoto of 90–135mm is known as the ideal portrait lens. It brings the subject in fairly close, but allows a little breathing space between you and them. Telephoto compression starts to take effect where distant objects begin to appear layered one on top of another. Depth of field becomes shallower and throws the background nicely out of focus on close subjects, such as people or flowers. This helps to isolate the subject and throw more importance on them. This focal length is good for removing ugly problems, such as litter or car parks in the foreground.

TELEPHOTO LENSES 150MM–400MM AND BEYOND

Telephoto compression and magnification really become apparent at these focal lengths. Buildings and mountains start to fall over one another to get to your lens!

Depth of field becomes almost non-existent, the longer the lens and greater the magnification, but this allows a subject to be sharply outlined against a very blurred background. A tripod should be used to allow for smaller apertures – this will give greater depth of field when required.

Digital SLR cameras with interchangeable lenses allow the use of ultra-long and fast telephoto lenses up to 1000mm. These are aimed mainly at professional wildlife and sports photographers, but allow staggering magnification of the subject. Camera shake is magnified proportionately so a very steady hand or a tripod is essential. Canon, Nikon and Sigma all produce Image Stabilizer lenses that use gyroscopic motors to reduce camera shake – yes, they do work!

Focusing

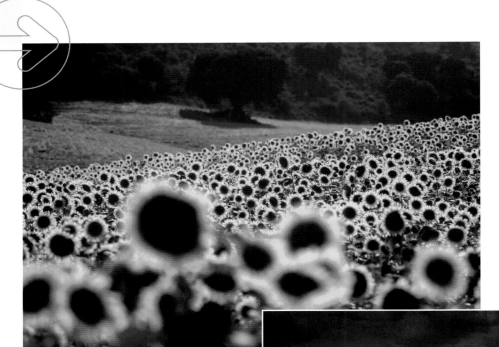

This is a perfect example of differential focusing. The foreground has been allowed to go out of focus on purpose in order to create an artistic effect. This is easier to achieve with a lens that is set to telephoto, as in this case, because the depth of field is less anyway.

TIP Learn to use manual focusing as it is always more reliable and precise in the long run, especially when you are taking photographs in low light.

Whether with fixed zoom or interchangeable lenses, digital cameras use auto-focus to control the focusing. On some models this can be switched to manual for tricky situations or when you want to override the camera. On the whole, technology has made auto-focus fast and reliable. Fast-moving action such as motor racing benefits hugely from it, but very few landscapes need fast auto-focus! Indeed, auto-focus is usually biased to the centre of the frame, and that is no good for many situations. Some cameras let you alter the bias from one area of the frame to the next, but manual focusing is often best for precise control.

Keep an eye out for times when your auto-focus system fails to work properly. In this case the wheat was very dark (it had to be lit with fill-in flash) and the lens struggled to find something to lock onto when focusing. Either focus and use the focus lock button or set the camera to focus manually, as I did here. Very dark or light scenes with little contrast between foreground and background are always going to fool the auto-focus, so learn how to focus manually. My camera is on manual focus all the time, unless I am shooting a fast-moving subject. You'll find that most mountains and cities stay quite still!

These shots show how the lens aperture affects the depth of field in a photograph. By gradually stopping down the aperture from f2 to f8 to f16 you can see that the zone of sharpness extends dramatically. This effect is a very powerful tool that can be used to great effect.

Hyper-focal focusing is a technique that relies on using the depth-of-field scale for maximum sharpness. If you have such a scale on your lens, move the infinity focus symbol on the right of the scale to where it displays your chosen aperture setting. This allows nearer objects to remain sharp. Depth of field covers two-thirds in front of your point of focus and one-third behind.

In practice, you can manually focus one-third of the way in, which usually gives adequate depth of field when used with a small aperture and wide-angle setting. If your camera does not have manual focus, it should have a focus lock button. This freezes the focus when pressed to let you recompose your shot.

Depth of field at longer focal lengths will be determined by the effect you desire. Choose a large aperture to create minimal depth of field. Long lenses and small apertures means you need a tripod for maximum sharpness, or camera shake will ruin the shot.

UNDERSTANDING DEPTH OF FIELD

Depth of field is the zone of sharpness in a photograph: the area before and after the point of focus at where the scene remains in sharp focus. Depth of field is controlled by your aperture setting, the focal length of the lens and the point of focus. The aperture is a diaphragm that controls the amount of light entering a lens and falling onto the CCD sensor. A large aperture of f2 will let in more light than a small aperture of f8. It also gives a smaller depth of field than a smaller aperture. The shorter the focal length, the greater the depth of field is. The longer the lens gets, the shallower the depth of field.

Any lens will have its maximum depth of field at infinity. The closer you get to a subject the more this reduces the depth of field. For the greatest depth of field use a wide-angle lens with a small aperture, and for minimal depth of field use a long telephoto lens with a wide aperture.

DIFFERENTIAL FOCUS

This technique is the opposite to hyper-focal focusing. Here the object is to create a deliberately narrow depth of field. This is done to put emphasis on the subject and throw the background totally out of focus. It is also a creative technique used for photographing relatively close-up objects such as flowers. Here close focusing makes the subjects deliberately large in the frame, and by using the widest aperture only a tiny part remains in detail. This is a very effective and artistic technique that works well on detail shots.

The longer the focal length is, the closer the focus; the wider the aperture, the more pronounced the effect becomes. Choose a small object to photograph, zoom in with the lens and use the widest aperture available to your lens. A tripod is often essential to allow precise focusing on one part of the subject. Try several shots, each with a smaller aperture and choose the one that pleases you the most.

Shooting close up to a subject will also allow differential focus to be used. Flowers are great for isolating tiny detail and letting the rest of the image go out of focus. Even when using small apertures, close-up (or macro) photography automatically reduces the depth of field, and depth of field diminishes the closer you get. You can sometimes end up with only a few millimetres in focus.

Exposure

You can't beat a good sunset. It's nature's dramatic end to the day. All the right ingredients were in place for a stunner – great clouds to add a sense of drama, water for reflections and the sun poking through the clouds just enough so that flare wasn't a problem.

Achieving the correct exposure for a shot is far from being an exact science. Often, it is far more useful to shoot a range of images at different exposures and then choose the best image at the editing stage. Here we highlight the different exposure techniques that are available to the photographer.

A fairly average shot that should cope well with any exposure mode. This is perfectly suited to matrix or centre-weighted metering. Here a polarizing filter was used to add extra impact to the sky.

Automatic exposure is perfectly acceptable for general shots, but understanding how exposures work and manually adapting the exposure will allow you to go that extra hurdle and create really stunning shots.

SPOT METERING

Here the camera uses a very narrow spot in the centre of the frame to analyse the light levels. This is a very accurate method of metering if you know where to point. Try taking a highlight and shadow reading and average them out. More sophisticated cameras will do the mathematics for you! You can also take a reading from a mid-tone area of the scene.

CENTRE-WEIGHTED METERING

A less sophisticated metering system that still works well for normal scenes. The whole scene is measured, with preference being given to the centre where the subject normally is. Point the camera away from extreme bright or dark areas and take an average of the scene.

MULTIPLE ZONE METERING

Multiple zone metering is the state-of-the-art metering system. The frame is divided into different zones (up to 256 in top digital cameras) and the light is measured from each zone with a bias to the centre of the shot.

GREY CARD

In-camera or hand-held reflected light exposure meters are calibrated to a standard 18% mid-tone grey reflectance from the subject. In theory, this will give a perfect exposure. This is fine if your subject is 18% grey, but most are not. You have to learn how to tweak the exposure reading of your camera in order to create a correct exposure.

A rough guide is to overexpose bright scenes by 1 to 1½ stops and bracket around this reading. The opposite is true when metering from dark subjects – in this situation underexpose by 1 to 1½ stops from the camera reading. Green grass, trees and mid-tone rocks/earth are all good for getting an average 18% grey reading.

TIP Learning to expose manually is a great advantage. Ultimately, this will enhance your ability to create the right mood for your shots, particularly in low-light conditions.

The contrast range in a shot doesn't get much higher than this: pure blacks next to pure whites. Here the camera tries to lighten the shot, turning it to 18% grey and ruining the lovely dark moody quality to the image. There are three options open to you for metering. First, take a reading from the dark area and decrease exposure by 1 to 1½ stops; second, take a reading from the highlights and increase exposure by the same amount; and third, take a reading from both areas and divide the two to get the right setting. 1/125 at f8 for the highlight, for example, and 1/60 at f8 for the shadows.

Exposure

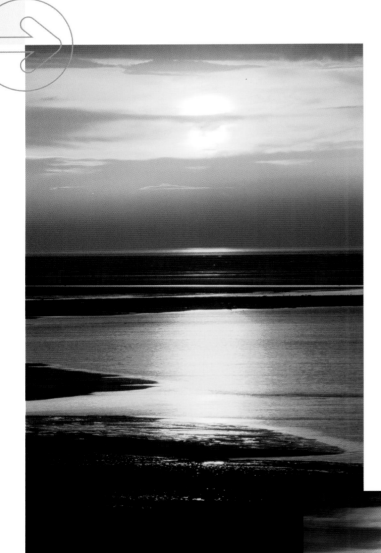

WHITE BALANCE

Tungsten lighting has a yellow colour cast. If you stand outside a house or shop you can see the yellow colour of the shop lights. Go inside and your brain will correct this effect.

The human brain can quickly adapt to various light sources and adjust them automatically to a more natural daylight effect. In essence, this is the same technique that digital cameras use to correct colour casts from artificial and natural light sources. Digital cameras use the white balance to correct any colour casts. It can be adjusted manually or automatically. The white balance becomes more critical under artificial lighting situations. The camera will adjust the light to be bluer under artificial lights. If you have daylight coming in through windows you will notice it goes very blue. This is similar to the old-fashioned technique of putting a blue filter over your lens.

As an experiment, try shooting a white sheet of paper in manual mode using the lighting conditions that you will be shooting under. This should give a fairly accurate colour correction. Some newer models will even bracket the white balance, giving a neutral, blue and red variation of the colour.

The three shots on this page illustrate bracketing. The correct exposure (shown here) was achieved by taking a meter reading to the side of the sun, keeping it out of the frame. I recomposed the shot afterwards.

Left to its own devices the camera meter will underexpose the shot and make it too dark (left). With overexposure there is more detail visible in the shore, but the light areas in the sky and on the relective surface of the sea blow out (right).

BRACKETING

Most digital cameras will allow you to bracket your shots by producing an under-, correct and overexposed version with one click of the button. You can then preview the variations and delete ones that don't work.

TIP With scenes that have areas of very strong contrast you can bracket several shots and use software to create a digital composite from the best bits of each, so creating the effect of one perfect exposure.

A classic shot that is often ruined by poor exposure. The highly reflective white snow causes underexposure, turning the snow grey. Simply remember to increase exposure by 1½ to 2 stops. You can dial this in using the exposure compensation dial on your camera.

FACT FILE

f-stops/apertures

The aperture in a lens through which light travels to the CCD plane is called the iris/diaphragm. It has been designed to open and close in incremental steps called f-stops. Most interchangeable lenses have full and half f-stop increments whilst most fixed zoom cameras will use 1/3 incremental steps for finer control. Expensive lenses usually have a larger aperture and therefore make faster shutter speeds possible. A lens with a maximum aperture of f2 will, for example, allow two stops' more light than a lens of f4. This is very useful in low light conditions.

APERTURE

Maximum										Minimum
f1.2	f1.4	f1.8	f2	f2.8	f4	f5.6	f8	f11	f16	f22
1/2000	1/1000	1/500	1/250	1/125	1/60	1/30	1/15	1/8	1/4	1/2

Shutter speeds (above in seconds)

Once the correct combination of aperture and shutter speed have been chosen for the exposure the following rule applies:
▶ One f-stop increase (from f4 to f2.8) admits double the light of the previous one, so the shutter speed has to be halved to compensate (i.e. 1/125 at f2.8).
▶ One f-stop decrease (from f4 to f5.6) admits half the light of the previous one, so the shutter speed has to be doubled to compensate (i.e. 1/30 at f5.6).

Automated exposure programs

These are built in programs that allow automated exposure, depending on which subject you are shooting.

Auto program (P)

The camera will choose the correct aperture/shutter speed for the exposure and will use stored exposure situations to come up with the best combination. You can usually change the aperture or shutter speed to suit your own requirements.

Shutter priority (S)

Enables you to set your desired shutter speed and the camera automatically selects the aperture for correct exposure. Shutter priority can be used to freeze fast-moving action or slow down the speed for blurred motion effects.

Aperture priority (A)

Enables you to set your desired aperture and the camera controls the best shutter speed for correct exposure. Aperture priority can be used to control depth of field. A large aperture will give shallow depth of field, while a small aperture will allow depth of field to be maximized for any given point of focus.

Low light

This seascape was shot at sunrise, where pre-dawn light is soft and full of colour. The challenge is working quickly, as the shift to daylight will spoil the effect.

This forest was shot at dusk, when the light takes on more colour. You can shoot until dark with a shutter speed of over 30 seconds, yielding interesting colour shifts as well.

Low-light photography is a technical challenge that seems quite daunting, but with experience will become a very important part of your repertoire. Generally, low-light levels occur after the sun has gone down but there are many days when the general light levels are low, especially during the winter.

The first challenge may be to get an exposure reading in the first place. If you are having trouble, open up the lens to maximum aperture and then take a reading. For every f-stop you close down you must double the exposure. If you close down 3 stops from a reading of, say, 5 seconds at f2.8, your new reading will be 10 seconds at f4 and finally 20 seconds at f5.6.

Night-time shots are the most difficult to pull off, with noise levels a major problem. This is a grainy effect noticeable in shadows and is caused by a lack of sensitivity in the CCD to pick up and record information in dark shadow areas. Newer cameras use various techniques, such as double exposures and a built-in noise reduction mode, to compensate for this; they also have more sensitive CCDs with a higher dynamic range. Landscapes need light in order

to see them – but how much light? The afterglow of a sunset can last for 30 minutes or so and leave enough light to record if you adopt long exposures. How long an exposure will depend on the subject and its reflectance values. Photographing deep within a forest can leave you struggling with long exposures even during the day. Most landscape subjects will have limited time before the exposure times become unmanageable.

CALCULATING EXPOSURE TIMES

Exposing for low-light does not need to be scary. Use the averaged camera exposure as a starting point. Also, bracket your exposures, as camera meters can often be fooled into underexposure. Usually you will only need to bracket to longer exposures, as underexposure is rarely a problem in these conditions.

Taking photographs in low light levels unfailingly creates mood and impact. Find the right subject matter and you can't fail to take stunning shots. In these pictures, I used car headlights for an unusual effect.

The impact of this beautiful mosque in Marbella, Spain was enhanced by shooting it at dusk, when it was also lit up by electric lighting to add to the drama. I made sure that the sky still retained some colour for added contrast, to bring out the detail of the silhouetted palm trees and the tall, narrow poplars in the background.

TIP → Always carry your tripod so that it can be put to use at a moment's notice. Having the right equipment to hand is essential for success.

ISO SETTINGS

The ISO setting on your camera allows you to change the sensitivity of the CCD so that you can use faster shutter speeds at low light levels.

Unlike conventional film, where you had to change the entire film to alter the ISO sensitivity, you can change the ISO setting on a per shot basis with digital cameras. The snag is a loss of quality, the higher the ISO setting you use. Extra noise and some colour shifts are possible side-effects. If you then use a compressed file format other than RAW/TIFF you will add to these quality problems. These are correctable, but for top quality use the finest ISO setting (usually ISO 100) and steady the camera for long exposures (digital photography still entails lugging a tripod around, I'm afraid!).

The top picture was shot 15 minutes after sunset, with a polarizer used to boost colour saturation in both sky and land. The lower shot, of the 'white village' of Olvera, Spain, was taken as the last rays of the sun hit the town. The colours are created by the natural beauty of the evening sunlight.

Using flash

Flash is rarely used in most landscape shots, but there are instances when a burst of fill-in flash can help to liven up a scene. There are two main options open to you for flash photography: using a built-in camera flash or appending additional external flashguns.

Built-in flashguns can fill-in a dark foreground subject and make it brighter if it is close enough, but they do have limitations because they are not overly powerful. Their main use will be to illuminate a subject such as flowers, which are close enough to the camera to be affected by the flash. Most flashguns have a range of approximately 0.5m to 4.0m (1.7 ft to 13 ft), which means that distant landscapes cannot be lit by the camera's built-in flash. Modern built-in flashguns will usually calculate the exposure for you. If you buy an additional flashgun for your camera (which can often be linked by an extension cord for greater freedom) stick to the same manufacturer, as most cameras will be able to communicate with these to maintain accurate flash exposures.

It is possible to produce some exciting shots if you have access to a more powerful hand-held flashgun that can be moved around independently of the camera. This can be used for a technique called 'painting with light'.

This is best suited to low-light photography so you have ample time to build up the flash with multiple exposures. Set the camera up on a tripod and set to either your longest exposure or multiple exposure, if your camera has this function. A multiple exposure facility will make this technique much easier as it allows you to re-expose the same frame again and again and build up a much greater flash effect.

With the camera shutter fired, you can then operate the flash as many times as you want within the length of exposure chosen. Some

The use of fill-in flash can add graphic impact to a shot and will reduce unwanted shadows. Objects which are close to the camera will need smaller apertures than wide angle shots, which will need wide apertures.

▤ *Here my car headlights were shone onto the boats, for added detail in the shadows. This kind of improvised lighting can give extra dimension and lift to a shot.*

▤ *Notice how the fill-in flash falls away in the background due to insufficient flash power, though it has actually created an interesting effect in this case.*

cameras will expose for several minutes, which is plenty of time to fire off numerous flashes. It is best to run about the scene and fire from different locations. Don't put yourself between the flash and the camera or it will record your silhouette. Try hiding behind objects in order to avoid this.

For every f-stop you close down your lens, the flash output has to be doubled to maintain the same exposure. For this reason it is best to use a wide aperture. Only experimentation with your own flash set-up will tell you the optimum aperture. Once this has been found, you can keep using the same aperture again and again.

Using several flashguns simultaneously is going to give greater flexibility and allow the flash exposure to be built up a lot more

quickly. Most flashguns can be fired remotely by attaching a slave unit via a cord. Place this slave so that it can see your main flash, and when you fire your main flashgun, it will automatically fire the remote flashgun. Flashguns are expensive, so look out for some second-hand ones.

'IMPROVISING' FLASH

Alternative light sources are car headlights. I have successfully placed my car so that the beam illuminates the subject. Car headlights offer a very powerful light source to experiment with. You can also try a powerful hand-held torch and paint with light: literally move the torch around during the long exposure so that the main subject is evenly illuminated all over.

▤ *These cosmos flowers in South Africa were given a burst of fill-in flash from a Metz 45 - hand-held flash unit. This has helped to* *brighten them against the stormy sky. I underexposed the shot by 1 stop, which has by default darkened the sky, adding to the effect.*

Scanning

Although this book is primarily aimed at people who have just bought a digital camera, you may, like me, have a cupboard full of old prints, film negatives and transparencies. How do you deal with these? There are two basic methods of digitizing these – using a flatbed scanner or a dedicated film scanner.

Flatbed scanners are more versatile, and some include a built-in transparency hood. At 2400ppi you get excellent results.

Film scanners are designed specifically to scan negatives, slides and transparencies at very high resolutions.

FILM SCANNERS

Film scanners are not cheap, but have come down in price enormously in recent years. Most scanners are made for scanning 35mm film and will do a very good job. The top-of-

TIP Warped negatives/ transparencies can be placed in a slide mount to improve sharpness. Tape them down as well.

the-range scanners can scan at 4000dpi or more and usually come with some form of filter software that automatically removes scratches and dust.

Dynamic range is also an important consideration when purchasing a film scanner. Most cheap film scanners start at 3.0, but 3.4 to 3.8 is the norm for a decent scanner. Top-of-the-range film scanners go up to 4.0 and beyond and will capture very dense shadow detail and bright highlights. A transparency film has an average dynamic range from 3.0 up to

3.6. A scanner with a smaller dynamic range suffers from blown out highlights and very dark shadows often coupled with noise, as they cannot capture the wide contrast range. If using a cheaper film scanner, try to scan slightly overexposed shots for best results.

If you only need to scan a few shots it may be more economical to use a system such as Kodak Photo CD. Here you send off your transparencies and Kodak will put them onto a CD that you can open up in an application such as Adobe Elements.

72dpi

100dpi

200dpi

A good scanner is a wise investment, but – as with digital cameras – resolution is a key issue. The higher the resolution of your scanner, the higher the resolution of your image, and the larger it can be printed without any loss of detail.

FLATBED SCANNERS

If you have film negatives you can use a film scanner or get them printed and use a flatbed scanner. Flatbed scanners are now very cheap and economical to buy, and even budget scanners offer good-quality scans. It is worth doing research first as this is such a vast market, but Epson, Microtek and Agfa all do top-quality flatbed scanners. Some flatbed scanners even come with a transparency hood that allows you to scan both slides and negatives. Try to get a flatbed with a dynamic range of 3.0 or more and a resolution of 2400ppi.

A flatbed scanner with a transparency hood that has a dynamic range of 3.6 or more is a serious piece of kit. It allows negative/transparency film and prints to be scanned to a high standard. It also lets you do experimental scanning with three-dimensional objects. Try scanning shells and using them in photomontages. Always use a protective glass/plastic sheet between the object and scanner.

RESOLUTION

Don't be deceived by flatbed scanners that seem to offer very high-interpolated resolutions. They are similar to digital cameras and the digital zoom/optical argument. Always go by the optical resolution. Higher resolutions are created by clever software, but it's not as clever as having the real power of optical resolution!

BIT DEPTH

The scanner's ability to record colour and tonal detail. The greater the bit depth, the better the quality will be. Digital cameras work at 8 bits per channel (3 channels RGB = 24 bits in total), while some scanners work at 10, 12 or even 14 bits per channel. Software packages such as Adobe Elements convert all images to a default setting of 24 bits.

TIP Warm the flatbed scanner up for 20 minutes beforehand or you may get strange colour casts appearing because the light source is still too cold. I normally let it do several pre-scans to warm it up.

This example illustrates how problems can develop in a scan and in images captured by digital cameras. It is caused by lack of sensitivity in the dynamic range of the camera/scanner. This results in a build-up of unwanted artefacts called noise. It usually occurs in the darker areas where less sensitive CCDs struggle to pick up all the subtle shadow detail. It may also occur in the highlights, but the problem there is that the detail blows out to white.

This series of images demonstrates how increasing resolution improves the detail visible in a shot. Remember that resolution is the key to good-quality scans and prints. For Web use a resolution of 72–100ppi; for email use 100–300ppi (only use 300ppi if you have fast broadband access, or download times will be very long); for printing use 300–400ppi.

300dpi

400dpi

2 Taking great landscape shots

Landscapes have long been one of man's great artistic themes, whether captured on canvas with paint or on film with a camera. Nature's beauty, colour and infinite variety will always inspire us. Film and high-street prints may have disappointed you in the past, seeming somehow to lose the magic of the moment, but with the control of digital photography you can capture – and even improve upon – what you see.

Capture the moment

 The difference that a few minutes can make! One minute I was despondent that the day was lost to grey, overcast weather conditions and the *next the sun popped out, albeit for a few minutes. Just enough time to grab a shot. I used a grey grad filter over the lens to maintain detail in the now stormy sky.*

TIP Some of the best landscape photographs are shot just after a storm has cleared. Dust settles, the air is fresh and the sky can create some amazing colours.

B eing in the right place at the right time is a skill that cannot be taught. To do this simply takes a great deal of time, patience and perseverance – and not a little bit of good fortune as well. But don't be deterred: stick at it and the results will pay dividends.

Photography is about freezing a fleeting moment in time. Blink an eye or turn your head and it's gone for ever. I find it quite depressing that somewhere I'm missing a beautiful shot, but you can't be everywhere all the time. Which is why you must make the most of the time that you do have whilst you are out photographing.

Preparation and planning will take you a long way down the road to capturing a successful photograph. Reading books, postcards and local literature will let you find the local beauty spots very quickly when travelling and allow you plenty of time to concentrate on and assess good viewpoints for shots.

If the weather is not right, use the time to reconnoitre the area and work out what time of day will work best for the shot. A compass is an invaluable aid in determining where the sun sets or rises. Always remember that sunset times vary with the seasons and the longitude, so don't get caught out by arriving too late for the shot because your brain is still running on summer time.

Patience is the most important weapon in a photographer's arsenal. I've lost count of the number of missed shots that just didn't happen because of bad weather or because I got bored waiting. When you have waited for what seems like an eternity and the sun does pop out from behind a storm cloud, it is a revelation to the soul. This is one of the most uplifting experiences a photographer can have.

Low sun is great for strong backlit scenes such as this one in a local park, where raking shadows fall across the land. You can't always get away to exotic locations, and exploring your own back yard can yield shots that are just as satisfying, and you can shoot in interesting light more often as you can get on location quicker. Here I used a soft focus and warm-up filter to add impact.

Remember to dress for maximum comfort, depending on the season, for you will not feel inclined to wait if too wet or cold.

One ugly stormy day in Spain I was driving around a mountain road. It was grey and miserable, but as I rounded the bend the sun popped out and I witnessed one of the most awesome sunsets of my life. The colours changed from pinks to orange to yellow. I was so engrossed with the shot that I forgot I was being soaked to the skin! Unpredictable weather is often the most exciting time to be shooting. It will usually be too horrible to shoot, but when the opportunity arises you can't beat it.

All of this will allow you to be in the right place at the right time to click the shutter and walk off with a winner.

FACT FILE

Making life easier

If you can park your vehicle close enough to your viewpoint, you can set up your tripod and composition and then wait in the comfort of your car, while only your tripod gets wet and cold. You don't always need to suffer for your art!

When the sun pops out, remember that the aperture will need to be 1 or 2 stops smaller to stop overexposure if you are exposing manually.

Cover your camera with a clear plastic bag in the rain, held in place with rubber bands, or buy an all-weather protective housing. Always remember to wipe down your camera gear with a cloth if it gets wet.

The sun lit up this Spanish finca or farmhouse as a break in the clouds appeared. This can be a frustrating time and patience is the key. You can often watch the sun as it moves closer, only to fizzle out at the last minute. I have waited for hours on occasion.

This is one of my most memorable sunsets shot in Spain. As I came around a corner in dismal rain the clouds parted to reveal this amazing shot. It is natural, not filtered in any way, and the scene changed colour several times.

These two shots show how the scene suddenly changes after the sun has disappeared. I like both shots, as they have very different yet equally valid moods. The blue shot, where the sun has disappeared is quieter and more reflective than the warmer, more vibrant sunny shot. Shoot under different lighting conditions to see the way colour changes throughout the day and use this to your creative advantage.

Composition

The pier was shot from below at low tide with a 35mm lens just as the sun was setting. I used a blur filter in Elements to soften the image for a moody effect.

This shot was taken with a telephoto lens. Note how the compression effect has filled the background with sand, and how the sun gives a beautiful backlit effect.

In addition to a beautiful location bathed in gorgeous light, the next most important ingredient in a photograph is the photographer's ability to compose the shot properly. Poor composition will ruin even the best conditions that nature can place before us.

Knowing how and where to point your camera will increase your success rate dramatically. Because composition is a matter of personal taste, this is possibly the most difficult technique to master. All composition is based around there being a frame beyond which you cannot see. The secret to good composition is the art of filling this frame with a subject to create a harmonious group of elements that are pleasing to the eye. Fail to make a good composition and the eye is left to wander aimlessly around the picture, as it has no principal focal point. Clever composition can also help us to imagine what lies beyond the edge of the frame.

KEEP IT SIMPLE

The first basic rule is to keep it simple. Don't clutter the shot with too many elements until your confidence in composing grows. Less is definitely more! The secret is to remove any distracting elements from the frame. Indeed, placing only the subject in the frame is the best way to bring prominence to it. This may be a barn or farm on top of a hill, or a wall and gate in the foreground, or a combination of the two. Including other distracting elements at the side will weaken the shot considerably.

RULE OF THIRDS

There is a rule that aids in creating consistently good composition. Based on what the Greeks called the 'Golden Section' and Leonardo called 'Divine Proportion', it is entitled the 'rule of thirds' and was originally created to make classical Greek architecture look more

TIP It is advisable to wear rubber wellington boots and use a tough camera bag when shooting in sandy, salty or dusty conditions.

TAKING GREAT LANDSCAPE SHOTS

These three shots show how very different results can be achieved by arriving at different times of the day and viewing a location from different angles. Getting to know a subject by repeat visits is a good exercise.

beautiful. Basically, you need to mentally split the composition up into thirds horizontally and vertically. Placing your subject where any of the lines intersect will, in theory, produce a harmonious balance. But remember that rules are there to be broken as well! There are many variables, and as film isn't at a premium there should be no excuses.

SHAPE AND FORM

All landscapes have shape and form, and your composition should help to bring out the best in them. Look out for strong shapes, such as circles, squares, rectangles and triangles. Triangular or diagonal shapes are amongst the strongest and most dynamic shapes that you can find, particularly when used to split a shot into two or more zones of interest. Use shapes in a bold manner to add impact to your shots. Remember that colour itself can create shapes, so use it to add power.

FOREGROUND / BACKGROUND INTEREST

It is important in most shots to have some form of foreground interest. The foreground may be the actual subject, with the rest of the shot being used as a background; or it may be used to draw the eye towards a subject further back in the frame. It is important to balance the lighting and composition between the two areas. Foregrounds don't always have to have a prominent area of interest and importance. Open spaces such as deserts create their own context by having nothing in them. This very emptiness therefore becomes the subject. Usually, such shots rely on textures being lit by a sun low in the sky – light and form in harmony without distractions.

Foreground interest also brings out a feeling of depth. This is partly due to foreground perspective, whereby a nearer rock is clearly bigger than one of a similar nature further

back in the scene. This is called diminishing scale perspective. Depth and scale within the picture are created by our own awareness of the relative size and shape that objects should be in the real world. Our brain is the storeroom for thousands of experiences; it uses these to work out what is going on in the shot. For example, an overhanging branch in the foreground with a small tree in the background gives a sense of depth. This is often called overlapping perspective.

Aerial perspective gives a feeling of depth by masking part of the landscape with fog, haze or mist. Areas closest in will have little or no mist and appear strong and vibrant. Thus depth is created by dark tones in the foreground, with light tones receding into the distance.

The background (usually skies) should also not be overlooked. Ideally, a photograph should have a perfect balance between foreground and background.

This late afternoon shot was made with a wide-angle lens and has caught the pier at its best with strong dynamic shadows bringing out texture in the wood and railings. If you look closely, you'll notice the sky was mirrored as it had blown out on the right hand side. The lamp was placed in the centre to create a sense of symmetry and the sky placed on the third.

Composition

A low angle has accentuated the drama of these rocks and reduced the impact of the slightly cloudy sky.

By using a car and my feet I managed to explore a large area of this lagoon and take photographs it from several different angles during the course of one day.

LEAD-IN LINES

This is a handy trick, which uses the natural perspective of receding or converging lines to create foreground interest. Often, a strong triangular, three-dimensional shape is formed when two lead-in lines are used, such as in a bridge, path, river, fence, ploughed field, road or wall. The long endless road running on for ever to the distant horizon is a classic example of the power of lead-in lines. The spot where the road eventually diminishes into nothing is known as the vanishing point.

LENS CHOICE

Depending on your lens choice, composition and focal point will change. Use a wide-angle lens for all-encompassing vistas. In general, the wider the lens, the greater the sense of depth and scale. If there are many layers in the frame, such as rolling hills, these will often give enough impact to carry the shot off on their own. Use the telephoto setting to isolate these parts of the landscape. It can also be used to remove unwanted foreground clutter, or to make your chosen subject matter more prominent within the shot.

PICTURE/IMAGE FORMAT

The most basic choice to make is: should you shoot horizontally (landscape) or vertically (portrait)? The most common format is landscape because the camera is designed with

a horizontal viewing screen. Try using the portrait format for a whole day as an exercise to aid your compositional skills. Portrait shots suit tall, elongated subjects like trees.

It is possible on the computer to crop the basic frame top and bottom in order to create a wide but short panoramic format, or to zoom in tight to crop out unwanted detail. For maximum success, this will require top-quality files saved at the highest resolution that your camera is capable of. Cropping a small but highly compressed file will have disappointing end results, as the resolution will be too poor.

SYMMETRY

Symmetrical landscapes are not uncommon and provide an excellent opportunity to create new and interesting variations on the usual compositional rules. Look for lakes, rivers, sea or any form of water or puddle. The main key to success is that the water must be perfectly still for maximum impact. Any wind blowing across the water and breaking it up into waves or ripples will ruin the shot. Sometimes very slightly off-centring the shot will lead to greater success. In this way, more emphasis may be given to the subject rather than to its reflection.

All the shots on these two pages were taken in one place – Knysna Lagoon, South Africa. Exploring the lagoon has yielded photographs showing many variations in the landscape of this one relatively small area.

This side of the lagoon was a nature reserve and a boat was needed to gain access to it. The upper shot was taken from the top of the cliff, where the views were amazing. On the way back down to the boat I walked along the beach and used the rocks as foreground interest to lead the eye into the sweep of the lagoon (lower picture).

Changing your viewpoint

Changing your viewpoint can have a dramatic effect on your shot. Just by walking around your subject you can find many different angles to shoot from, all giving a new and interesting interpretation to the subject.

New photographers tend to remain static at their chosen location. They take a couple of shots near the car park. By stepping back from the shot and walking around, you can discover much more potential to your subject. Sometimes you may have to work very hard to get a good viewpoint. Be prepared to do some walking up steep hills!

Lowering the angle of viewpoint by tilting the camera or crouching down will give a dramatic increase to the feeling of apparent depth, especially with a wide-angle setting on your lens. This is a good way of avoiding having a boring sky in the frame. It also allows you to concentrate on the foreground interest that is going to be your main subject matter. Good depth of field is essential in almost all cases, so use a tripod and watch out for any shadows that have been cast by you.

Getting up high is another means of changing your viewpoint. But looking down will not generally give you the same sense of foreground drama as choosing a viewpoint low to the ground. If you get up really high, this will allow sweeping panoramas to be taken. Often, though, simply standing on a brick wall can lift your shot above the ordinary.

Looking up at tall buildings can give an exaggerated sense of perspective known as converging verticals. Architectural purists may frown on this, but such a viewpoint often allows dynamic compositions to be created.

Framing

Choosing how to frame a scene can make or break a photograph. A good sense of composition is absolutely essential. Fortunately, digital photography allows photographers to recompose their pictures at their leisure on the computer desktop. This can enable you to transform a good photograph into a great one, given the right subject matter.

A good compositional trick is to look for something to frame your subject, such as a tree or archway. This is a great way of placing emphasis on your subject. Framing a subject can give it an air of mystery, as though you are peering into a place from a hiding position. It can also help to cement the subject within the landscape and give a shot more impact. Always keep an eye out for different ways to interpret your subject. Spend time looking and walking around your subject to find the different possibilities that unfurl as you view it from different perspectives.

Using a natural frame can help to hide any ugly and distracting areas that would otherwise ruin the shot. A car or a boring sky can be effectively removed from the composition without weakening it. If no natural frame is available it is still possible to add a frame later on in Adobe Photoshop

The original shot was a good mixture of texture and light. I removed the inside of the arches, then put the farm on a new layer behind the archway.

The tree was used to create a frame around the poppies in the background. I used a telephoto setting and tripod for sharpness.

Both natural and man-made frames can add an extra dimension to your shots. Always keep an eye out for features that make strong frames and keep a variety of shots on file for use in photographs where a good frame is lacking.

Elements or other software package. It beats having to rip off a branch and dangle it in front of the lens to hide an eyesore – an old pre-digital trick!

It is worth keeping a file of useful shots that can be employed at a later stage. Frames can often be found when the shot's actual subject matter is of little use. Using Photoshop Elements, it is possible to select the frame, cut it out, and use it in another shot. Take several shots with different focal lengths and angles so that a good choice is available.

You must remember to keep a balance between the foreground and the subject, so as not to make the frame too dominant in the

shot. Don't let the subject become too small by using your lens at too wide an angle. Instead, move back and use the middle range of your zoom lens to slightly compress the perspective, thus making the subject naturally bigger.

Depth of field can be altered to place emphasis on the frame or the background. A tree, for example, can be made the focal point and the background made out of focus using a telephoto and a large aperture, allowing the shape of the tree to dominate the shot. Alternatively, focusing on the background can make the tree out of focus, drawing the eye into the shot. Both can be kept in focus with a long exposure if a suitable support is available.

TIP Choose a frame with similar lighting, and with sunlight coming in from the same direction. You can always flip one of the images in Elements from left to right or vice versa.

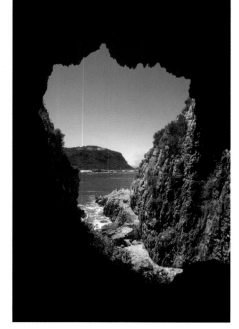

The palm leaves in this Florida sunset become both the frame and the subject of the picture at the same time. Again, I zoomed in for a tight crop, *which emphasizes the shapes of the leaf silhouettes. Meanwhile, careful positioning of the sun behind a leaf stopped flare from ruining the shot.*

The palm trees were used here to create a simple frame around the church. I chose the angle and moved backwards behind the trees to place the *church carefully between two palm leaves. This takes thought at the time, but you'll get extra Brownie points for such careful attention to detail!*

Shooting from inside a cave created a naturally occurring frame. I made sure that the subject wasn't lost in a mass of dark edges. The exposure *of the sea was taken before entering the cave and was entered as a manual setting. I then bracketed several shots either side of this reading.*

Focal points

Most landscapes should have what is known as a focal point within the image. This is usually the subject and the main point of interest within the composition. Without a focal point most landscapes suffer from 'wandering eye syndrome'. That is, the eye wanders around the frame aimlessly trying to find some relevance to the shot.

The focal point in a shot is usually obvious – it is probably the thing that drew your attention to the shot in the first place. It may be an isolated group of trees in a desolate landscape, a farm on a hill, a boat on the sea or a dramatic rock formation. It may even be a small element within the frame, but it will be strong enough to bind the whole composition together. The focal point often gives the picture a sense of scale. If you have a large expanse of sand, one tiny dot of a person can suddenly add meaning to the shot. By using all the other compositional aids you can create strong dynamic shots time after time.

DETAIL

Don't forget that many lenses can focus down to a short distance. Often referred to as macro photography, this is a valuable ally. It allows a range of images taken at close (but not microscopic) distance. Many modern lenses can focus down to these levels, making it a shame to waste their potential.

Many details await the photographer in the world of macro. Although it is not a traditional landscape photograph as such, you should always keep an eye out for interesting shots. Close-ups of flowers can produce captivating images. Use minimal depth of field by opening up the aperture, and some beautiful shots can be achieved. The next step is to turn that fleeting sensation into a viable photograph.

Here the house is clearly the point of interest, but its diminutive size leaves you feeling how small mankind is compared to nature. Rocks have been used to create foreground interest leading the eye down to the farm.

Symmetrical patterns occur frequently in nature, but not usually in quite such a regimented form as these rows of trees. Any type of repetition can be an interesting subject to photograph. Good side lighting is often an essential requirement.

If this shot had been taken on a dull day the effect would have been diluted considerably. The intense blue offsets the barren land perfectly. A small group of trees on the third anchors the whole shot together.

Picking out detail from the general scene can simplify design and composition, allowing you to focus on one specific element. Placing your camera on a tripod allows you to let it wander around the scene. Focus and compose at leisure.

Getting in close to a subject can reveal new and often exciting areas of discovery. Nature is often revealed in its full glory when you zoom in close. Most lenses will have some form of macro ability – that is, the ability to focus very close to a subject. Check the camera for lens specs before you buy. Combine a wide focal range with the ability to focus closely and you can take advantage of various photographic opportunities.

It's always a good idea to look where you're walking! I nearly walked straight past this group of frozen bracken leaves. The frost has left a beautiful design all over the leaves. Getting in closer has helped to reveal this fine detail. A steady hand or tripod is a must to maintain the intricate patterns when printed.

TIP → Macro shots will suffer from even the slightest camera shake, just as long telephoto shots do. Both are highly magnified. Use a suitable support to avoid having them ruined by blurring.

As the sun moved around, I saw the statue was going into shadow, allowing me to take the silhouette. I returned an hour later after taking some other shots.

Colour

Understanding colours and their relationships is fundamental to creating pictures with impact. The successful photographer will use the psychological effect of colour intelligently by juxtaposing harmonious and/or complementary hues to create the right emotion. The warmer, more animated harmonies of red and yellow create a feeling of summer. Colder, more subdued blues and violets remind us of winter. These qualities can be used to alter the mood of a shot.

This diagram shows where each colour lies on the colour wheel. Clashing colours lie opposite each other while harmonious ones lie side by side.

The lovely cool blue sky above Bodiam Castle in Sussex adds just the right amount of colour tension to the contrasting warm wood and bricks.

Colour helps create atmosphere and sets the tone of the entire image – a funfair, for example, exudes many clashing, vibrant colours that compete for attention. At the opposite end of the spectrum a moody, sombre, misty winter sunrise may exhibit the merest hint of colour and be almost monochromatic.

Knowing what to look for and how to take advantage of colour is essential to creating a successful photograph.

Light creates colour by absorbing certain wavelengths and reflecting others. All colours are made by mixing the three basic primary colours of red, blue and green. A yellow sunflower, for example, absorbs blue light; the green and red light reflected make the colour yellow.

This is also what happens at sunset when the sun is at a low angle and the atmosphere

Here the sunset has a single colour range of reds, yellows and oranges. It sends a clear, strong message about the warmth we associate with this end of the colour spectrum.

absorbs more blue light. Mixing equal amounts of all three will produce white light. Black is created when all colours are absorbed in equal amounts. Grey is also an equal amount of all three colours; a cool grey has a slight bias to the blue end of the spectrum. A TV monitor uses red, green and blue phosphors.

Although it's great to find perfect shots, digital manipulation allows for some wonderful, varied and precise effects to be achieved with minimal effort. Perfect digital colour harmony (or discord!) is only a mouse click or two away.

Colour is one of nature's greatest gifts. Each season brings with it a new way of seeing and using colour to create form and structure in the landscape.

In this shot the sun has recently gone down, leaving the shoreline bathed in beautiful warm colours. Capturing these colours in low-light conditions takes a wide aperture and a long exposure, but the result gives the scene a stunning sense of atmosphere.

WARM COLOURS

Reds, yellows and oranges are very strong, dominant colours – the colours of summer. They are the colours of fun and life. Red is also the colour of blood and a sign of danger, signifying the warmth of the sun and blazing fire. Because of this we perceive any object that is coloured as being hot.

The cold blue colour helps to set off the small amount of warm artificial tungsten lighting on this pier. The two contrasting colours create a disharmonious tension. In this case, the effect is subtle – the overall colour is biased to the blue end of the spectrum.

COLD COLOURS

Blues, violets and cyans are cold colours – the colours of winter. They are known as receding colours because the landscape gets cooler in colour towards the horizon. This effect can be used to portray a feeling of depth when warmer colours are used in the foreground. Dawn is often cooler than sunset; adding a blue colour cast to boost your shot will give a sense of tranquillity and calm. Cool colours create a sense of sadness and depression, which humans often feel when it's cold outside – hence the term 'feeling blue'.

This blue is totally different – it is the intense blue of a clear sunny day. The bright yet limited colour palette has led to a graphic shot that would not have worked at all on a dull day. Remember: white objects need careful exposure – try 1½ to 2 stops over the suggested meter reading to be sure.

Colour

NATURAL COLOURS

White is often associated with purity; it is what you might call a colourless colour. White is all colours combined. Snow evokes a feeling of isolation, cold and freshness, but is also used to give a modern feeling. Black, on the other hand, immediately creates a sombre, sad feeling.

Because nature creates most living plants in green, this colour is probably perceived as the most natural. It is nature's base colour; the colour of growth and fertility. Think of a field of fresh, cool green crops in spring and compare it to an empty hot arid desert. This is the power of colour in action.

PASTEL COLOURS

When colours are muted or desaturated, a pastel effect is created. Any colours can be used together quite successfully when muted. Fog and mist, for example, naturally help to desaturate and harmonize all colours. As we'll explain later in Chapter Three, image-editing applications, such as Adobe Photoshop Elements allow excellent colour control, so that even strong colours can be desaturated to create delicate colour effects. If necesary, you can also make use of filters to bring a shot to life. Adding a little noise, for example, can help to create atmosphere.

Chlorophyll, which creates the green colour inside plants, is the building block of life on Earth. It has to be one of the most natural and important colours in life! This shot encapsulates Mother Nature's most popular colour.

The sunset didn't quite happen on this occasion as it clouded over. I persevered and still came away with a nice shot, although not the one I was expecting! The cool blue colour is a natural phenomenon of overcast weather conditions in low light.

Here, in Death Valley, the temperature was formidable – it almost melted my camera! These are stark, almost monochromatic shots with minimal colour. If you find yourself in similar circumstances, try using a polarizer to reduce heat haze and glare.

Colour can be made to work in a whole variety of ways, depending on whether it is used aggressively, with great subtlety or somewhere in between. In the right hands it will add mood, atmosphere and power to a photograph.

Colour

◁ *A single red poppy has the ability to dominate a shot even when it is quite small – such is the power of the colour red.*

▽ *The red swathe of poppies in this shot is quite dominant in the foreground. Add a dramatic sky and sun and you have a*

winning visual combination. An ugly telegraph pole which would otherwise have ruined the shot was cloned out.

MONOCHROMATIC COLOURS

Colour photographs do not need to contain every colour of the rainbow to convey mood. Using one dominant colour with a secondary hue present can create an immediate and powerful effect. The narrowing of the visual spectrum allows the subject matter to become more dominant. Shapes and form take on a more important role in the power of the final image. Silhouettes can also work very well with monochromatic colours as they let you create a graphic interpretation of the subject.

COMPLEMENTARY COLOURS

Nature offers a world of colour in many different forms. There are two basic types of colour: complementary colours (yellow/violet, blue/orange, red/green), which are opposite each other on the colour wheel; and harmonious colours, which lie next to each other on the colour wheel. The primary colours red, green and blue are mixed to make up the secondary colours of yellow, cyan and magenta. By mixing equal quantities of red, green and blue, white light is created.

Complementary colours give maximum contrast, creating a jarring sensation when used together. This can be used to eye-catching effect in a shot. By making one colour more dominant in the picture, more subtle colour-contrast effects can be produced.

HARMONIOUS COLOURS

Colours that lie either side of each other on the colour wheel are considered harmonious. This is why green when mixed with yellow and blue creates a harmonious effect. This is the colour of a field of young green crops on a sunny day with a blue sky. A field of sunflowers is also harmonious, but if you darken the sky to a deep blue with a polarizing filter you begin to get more contrast. This is because the blue begins to enter the violet/purple end of the spectrum, which is opposite to yellow on the colour wheel.

FACT FILE

Colour detail
Sometimes colour can become the subject matter in a photograph. It may often be only a detail within a larger subject, so be prepared to tightly crop the composition. Removing the subject from its fuller context creates an abstract pattern, so be on the lookout for interesting textures and details within the wider picture. The telephoto end of your lens is ideal for capturing such shots.

Light

Shot after the sun had gone down, in this image the ambient light was fading quickly. All of the land has turned to shadow. The only detail left is in the highly reflective water.

This vantage point was reached in time to take a sunset. It was a moody affair that I tried to accentuate. It's difficult to fight the light, so go with the flow! A grey grad filter (see page 58) was used for an 'end of the world' effect.

Capturing the ever-changing quality of light represents a unique challenge for the photographer. As the sun rises and sets, it is possible to capture a range of different moods and feelings. How you choose to harness Mother Nature's natural lighting rig is totally up to you.

This low-key shot has hardly any highlight detail – just enough to show the texture and form of the sand. The sun was very low in the sky to get this shot. You do not want grey, so underexpose by 1 stop and then 1½ stops to keep the wonderful dark colours.

High-key shots are harder in landscapes because you don't have much control over the tones present in the land. Shooting in winter with snow on the ground helps to create a more high-key effect. You can alter the contrast range using Levels in Adobe Elements.

Undoubtedly light is the most important factor involved in a photograph. From the grandest vista to the smallest detail, light is the most valuable ally any photographer has.

Quality of light changes throughout the day and the seasons. It is also dependent on the weather conditions.

Early and late light creates the most drama. The strong directional side lighting is ideal for landscapes; it reveals texture, shape and form. As the sun rises, it becomes harsher and more contrasting and you lose the shadows that add all the drama. Photographs are still possible, but look out for more graphic shots where colour might play a more important role. Shooting in winter can give you the best light of all. Because the sun is low in the sky you get fantastic side lighting all day long.

Weather is also an important factor. Shooting on an overcast day will yield soft directionless light. This is great for portraits, but less so for landscapes. It is a good time to try black-and-white shots, but some subjects such as flowers with delicate detail work well in softer light. Adding a little sun to a stormy grey day will result in very dramatic shots.

HIGH KEY/LOW KEY

Knowing how your exposure system works will allow you to create a specific style of shot. Altering the exposure, along with considered thought as to the subject matter of your photograph and the type of exposure to which it is suitable, can give rise to surprisingly different moods.

HIGH KEY

High-key photography makes use of a restricted tonal and colour range. The image tends to portray a delicate, ethereal, two-dimensional quality and is predominantly made up of light tones. This should not be confused with a high-contrast image, which can include both pure black and pure white tones in the shot. A high-key image has a squashed tonal range of predominantly medium to light greys and whites.

The background should be bright and overexposed to add to the overall effect. It is often possible to combine elements of high key with those of high contrast, where the subject is predominantly made up of light colours, but there are small areas of dark tones in the shot.

Good subjects include landscapes and woodland scenes shot on misty days. The mist turns dark colours into pale colours. Combine the sun and a little overexposure and you can produce pleasing high-key landscape shots.

LOW KEY

Low-key photography produces completely the opposite feelings to high-key shots, but should not be confused with images that are low-contrast, which suffer from a lack of solid blacks. Low key is essentially a medium-to-high contrast image heavily biased towards a predominance of dark tones.

Dark, brooding, stormy landscapes lend themselves well to the low-key approach. Here, dark shadows and dark backgrounds help to create a shadowy, sombre, mysterious feeling with a three-dimensional effect. Generally speaking, there is far more subject matter to choose from, because most shooting situations will be in the medium-to-high contrast zones ideally suited to low-key photography.

The painter Rembrandt was probably the greatest master of low-key studies, using a technique called chiaroscuro in which objects are brought out strongly by the use of a dark background that is highlighted by brighter areas. Low-key is essentially a medium-to-high contrast image heavily biased towards a predominance of dark tones.

There are no hard-and-fast rules to shooting high-key and low-key shots and many times you will find there is a cross-over with another style or technique. Use it as a starting point and get creative!

The soft diffused light has helped to create a high-key effect here. The computer was used to lighten the shot.

This has a monochromatic effect, where one colour is dominant throughout the shot of the pier.

Time of day

Venture out on a dull, dreary day and the chances are you will get dull, dreary, boring shots. The secret to great shots is to be in the right place at the right time. Get the mix of light and subject matter right and you will almost definitely be assured of a great photo being exposed onto your CCD. Light is without doubt the photographer's most important tool. Knowing how and when to get the best out of the light will dramatically improve your shots overnight.

SUNRISE

This is the quietest part of the day when even the birds are not yet awake – if you can struggle out of bed in the middle of the night to be in position for daybreak, you will be rewarded with a tranquil yet inspiring experience. Weather is always the main bone of contention with landscape shots, so listening carefully to the weather report will give you an idea of what to expect. Pleasant weather conditions such as morning mist evaporating can create an unexpected atmospheric bonus.

As the night gives way to daybreak a soft landscape begins to emerge, in which shadows are weak and colours are muted and pastel in hue. The light is often clean and clear and on the cool side because atmospheric haze and pollution are at their lowest. Many advertising shots are done in this period because the light is soft and sensuous. This sunless light minimizes contrast problems and is ideal for bringing out maximum detail.

As the dawn sun breaks the horizon, the light changes very quickly. The world is flooded with soft warm light which races across the land, producing wonderful long shadows that create a 3-D effect and reveal texture and shape in the hills and valleys. In winter there are amazing contrasts between cool blue shadows and warm red highlights, leading to some amazing shots.

You will have about a 20-minute window of opportunity to grab light at its best, so you have to work fast and be in position or the moment will be lost. Your camera will also have to react because the exposure can change within seconds by several f-stops. Always keep an eye on the exposure and verify it for every shot you take. If you're shooting into the sun remember to take the reading without the sun, in the shot or underexposure will occur.

Sunrise is harder to work out where to position yourself than sunset, as you don't have the sun setting to give an approximation of where the light will strike first as it appears. Using a compass will give an idea of which way is east, but revisiting a good beauty spot is well worthwhile as intimate knowledge of the area will always help when scouting for the best spots.

The quality of light changes considerably during the day – from soft muted colours at sunrise, through harsh midday sunlight, back to soft colours at sunset. It also changes in colour, contrast, strength and direction as the sun tracks through the sky.

Early morning and early evening are ideal for landscape shots. In the time after sunrise and before sunset the warm, muted colours and soft light bring out the best from the scene.

The harsh light of midday maximises contrast and pushes colour saturation to the limit. With a strong scene and a simple, bold composition, this is still a good time to shoot.

MIDDLE OF THE DAY

Many photographers pack up for the day after shooting the sunrise, as the light becomes harsher and more contrasting. Although most landscapes work best at sunrise or sunset, good images can still be found. Colours are now fully saturated, especially with a polarizing filter, and the light is at its hardest with short featureless shadows. On these occasions the secret is to look for shots that these lighting conditions will enhance. Simple shots containing few elements work best. Although not set in stone, the old adage of shooting with the sun behind you often works best for maximum colour and graphic intensity.

LATE AFTERNOON/SUNSET

Like early morning, this is a good time for shooting landscapes – especially in an urban environment where buildings will benefit from strong side lighting. It is often called the Golden Hour – the sunlight has warmed up again as it descends to the horizon. The hour before sunset gives you perhaps the best part of the day. Shooting into the sun can give dramatic foreground silhouettes depending on the sun's intensity, but remember: don't look directly into the sun, especially through a telephoto lens, as eyes can be damaged. If possible, stop down the lens with a depth-of-field button or use sunglasses. A grey graduated filter is often useful to maintain a balance between sky and land. Even a digital camera has limitations to the amount of detail it can record.

DUSK/TWILIGHT

Don't pack up your camera just yet! Many interesting shots are to be had after the sun has disappeared. You now get the beautiful soft afterglow of dusk when the light is still glowing with warmth – very similar to the light of pre-dawn. Long exposures can turn the sea into an ethereal mist, while cities come alive. Watch the change in the mix of artificial and natural light happen over a half-hour period and keep on shooting every five minutes. In this case, dusk shots usually work much better than dawn shots because there are no lights on in the houses early in the morning. Keep shooting, using long exposures until the sky has gone black. A dark blue tint in the sky often compliments the warm colours of artificial lighting.

COLOUR TEMPERATURE

Measured in degrees kelvin, this is the scale by which colour is measured.

As the sun rises, its colour changes and this can be measured. Normal daylight is measured at $5,500^\circ$ K – this is when the sun is around the middle of the day and colours reflected off objects are deemed to be normal (i.e. a white object appears white with no colour cast). If you photograph at sunset the temperature drops to about $2,500^\circ$ K, which is a redder colour. The white object will now reflect a red colour. The human brain does a very good job of cancelling out this colour change, but the camera's CCD records a true image. The scene, therefore, will look warmer than you remember. This is generally not a bad thing, but you can alter the white balance to correct this if necessary. Such colour casts can be a problem if you are photographing inside a tungsten-lit room and you want the colours to look normal.

Different light sources also emit strong colour casts – mercury vapour lights are green and sodium lights are yellow. On the whole, it is best to correct any casts introduced in your image-editing software (*see page 84–91*).

TIP If you're shooting into the sun, take an exposure reading without the sun in shot – or your picture will be underexposed.

Contre jour

In this shot a grey grad filter (see page 58) was used to maintain detail in the white village. The village still needed to be brightened and the contrast was also boosted to balance the shot. Without the grey grad the village would have disappeared into a black shadow.

'Contre jour' is a fancy French term that simply means 'shooting into the light'. This technique cannot be achieved without some form of dramatic light, which you use to create moody, atmospheric shots. Create silhouettes by shooting into the light. For this you have to expose to allow for the bright light to turn any foreground interest into dark shadow. When the shape of an object is reduced to its bare outline, the resulting silhouette can create a fantastic graphic form. It really helps to bring out the profile of objects. This technique can transform ordinary-looking subjects into really strong visual statements.

Using reflectors or flash for fill-in light can give you the best of both worlds. Here you should choose a more detailed shot for your subject matter, as fill-in light has limited power, so large areas of landscape can't be lit properly. Backlight the subject as usual and use fill-in during the exposure. A reflector is an ideal means of reflecting light back into the subject because you can see the effect before pressing the shutter. Flash requires more experience and generally gives a less natural lighting effect.

Exposing for silhouettes is relatively easy. Most cameras actually produce perfect exposures by mistake. The exposure meter is fooled into underexposure by an overly bright dominant light source, which is exactly what you want. The severity of underexposure that you will need also depends on your subject. Strong shapes such as trees or buildings work well going completely black, but some, such as flower details, require bracketing to find the best exposure. Other subjects such as sunsets require you to override this exposure for correctly exposed shots.

One potential problem with this technique is lens flare. This is caused by light reflecting off internal glass elements within the zoom. Try to hide the sun behind your subject to reduce possible flare. When shooting backlit trees, for example, a single branch can be used. There is a fine line between flare and the starburst effect, where specular highlights turn into little stars. The lens diaphragm being stopped down causes this. With the sun behind a tree branch, try moving your camera a fraction and the tiny amount of controlled sunlight will turn into a starburst effect. In other instances, flare can be used creatively. Pixel-based software such as Adobe Photoshop Elements actually has its own lens flare filter to do the job in a controlled manner. Although bad flare is very difficult to retouch on the computer, small dots of flare can be eradicated quite successfully with the *Clone* tool.

Backlighting your subject allows you to create instant graphic images where the shape of the subject is important to the final impact of the shot. Using a grey grad filter allows you to keep detail in the shadows.

A classic silhouette where strong backlighting has rendered the pier a solid black. Simply meter from the sky to create this type of effect. Use the Levels *command to fine-tune the mid-tone and highlights later on before printing the picture.*

If shooting with the sun directly in the frame, try to partially hide it behind the subject to avoid bad lens flare problems. With the sun directly behind the palm tree, the camera has automatically under-exposed the image creating a silhouette.

This is taken from the series of shots made at one of my favourite sunsets in Spain. The sun is partially hidden behind cloud, so didn't flare too much in this shot. A meter reading was taken to the side of the frame to ensure that the bright sun didn't influence the meter into underexposing.

FACT FILE

Contre jour with landscapes

Shooting into the light can also produce dramatic wide-angle landscapes. The sun may pop out from behind a cloud during a storm to light the land. Here you may want to retain a balance between land and sky, so, if possible, use a grey grad filter to maintain detail in shadows and highlights. It may also pay dividends to shoot several exposures for highlights and shadows when the lighting and subject matter are very complicated. Use Photoshop Elements to put the shots in *Layers* and use the *Eraser* tool to get rid of darker or lighter areas.

This was shot very early one summer's morning at 4 a.m. London was fast asleep, apart from one person who called the police saying I was up to no good at that time in the morning on

Waterloo Bridge! Fortunately I was rewarded with a great sky for all my troubles. Notice how the office buildings aren't lit up at this time, and the different feel this gives to a cityscape.

Sunrise and sunset

For this shot, a pre-dawn start allowed me to take full advantage of the amazing hoar frost. I normally drive past these trees, but not this time – they looked fantastic. Unusual weather can make mundane sites seem special.

Shooting on cloudless days can lead to disappointing results, but a little mist or haze can lead to a beautiful pale orange sun hanging in the sky. You will need an interesting foreground subject to give more impact to the shot on such occasions.

There is nothing quite so breathtaking as a sunrise or sunset caught in its full glory. But catching it is not simply a matter of point and click – it takes time, patience and planning to keep pace with the sun. The photographer who is able to follow a few straightforward rules will be rewarded many times over.

Here the rocks and clouds have combined to create a strong composition. They almost mirror each other – the soft and hard textures of nature. The soft light of dusk also adds to the rich textures.

For the photographer, the most interesting light occurs in a narrow band just before and just after sunset or sunrise. Perhaps the most magical moment is when the sun is just about to appear from below the horizon or is just about to disappear for the day. The sun is at its lowest and casts wonderful long shadows, and where the sun hits water it creates a long shimmering beam of golden light.

Sunrise is a much quieter affair than sunset. Often, the land is eerily still, without even the birds moving or making any noise. It is usually colder because the land has cooled down during the night. In good weather conditions you will either be greeted with crystal-clear light or mist and fog formed during the night. Clouds are a godsend as they add lots of drama to the sky, and will take on the beautiful fiery colours of the sun when it is just above or below the horizon. Take plenty of shots as the sun and clouds interact. The light and colour will change continuously, so be ready.

Sunsets are warmer, due to more pollution and haze being present in the sky at the end of the day. Clouds are also more interesting and livelier as the sun has warmed them up over the day, producing faster-flowing and more changeable formations.

Getting up from a warm cosy bed at the crack of dawn is difficult, especially in the winter, but it can lead you to some of your most memorable photographic experiences and one or two cracking shots in the bag as well.

Shooting with a telephoto, I just managed to grab the last remnants of the sun going down. The sun sets remarkably quickly when you stop and time it. You have to be able to set up your shot quickly if you arrive on the scene late.

The groyne jutting out into the sea, the pebbles in the foreground and the slow shutter speed have made this shot. The groyne creates tension within the composition, being placed at an angle to the horizon.

TIP Having tried it, I know for a fact it is impossible to chase a sunset unless you own a jet plane! Pre-planning your location is necessary for successful shots.

This was shot whilst with my parents in Marbella, Spain. I'm glad I remembered to take my camera and tripod along! It needed several seconds' exposure, which would not have been possible with a hand-held camera.

FACT FILE

Silhouettes

Making a silhouette with a sunset is easy. Most foreground subject matter will automatically come out jet-black in these conditions because the camera's meter will underexpose when there is such a bright-point light source.

Silhouettes can produce very strong graphic images that look great blown up big and framed on the wall. To keep detail, try using a grey grad filter over the sky and take a meter reading to the side of the sun so that it isn't in the frame. Keep an eye out for strong shapes that will work well as silhouettes. Look out for bold, simple lines that are going to be immediately recognizable.

Night photography

Night is one of my favourite times: you've just taken a great sunset, then you wait for light levels to fall for a night shot. Two for the price of one – my kind of deal!

Fireworks are a great subject – technically they are a little demanding, but good fun to shoot. A tripod is absolutely essential for success as exposures are quite long. Some foreground interest can help to balance the shot and show where the event took place.

Any camera and lens will suffice, but a tripod is an absolute must for successful night shots. You might think of night as a black sky, but the real secret to good photographs is to shoot at twilight. Also known as the crossover period, it is the time when light and colour are still in the sky, but the sun has gone and any artificial illumination starts to become visible.

Find a subject such as an old building that is properly lit and you have hit the jackpot with almost guaranteed success. The best technique is to choose one location and shoot it over the entire twilight period until there is no colour left in the sky. This will allow you to see how the mix of light affects the overall picture. As it gets darker and the exposure gets longer, very bright

buildings can cause hot spots that will severely overexpose or 'burn out'. Shooting at shorter exposures to compensate will underexpose the sky and shadows to black, which usually looks awful. It is difficult to predict with accuracy the optimum point when all the different light sources are in balance, so keep on shooting!

One technique to try is to merge several shots together on the computer, steal the highlights from a bright building and put them in a shot where the general exposure is fine except for the burnt-out highlights. Exposures for night shots are not difficult. Use the average camera exposure as a starting point. Then bracket your exposures, as camera meters can be fooled into underexposure.

These two shots were taken within 15 minutes of each other, and highlight how important it is to keep shooting for as long as you can. Don't put the camera away until the sky has gone pitch black.

ACCESSORIES

Some form of cable release is essential, as trying to hold down the exposure button by hand for 30 seconds will usually result in camera shake ruining the shot.

COLOUR CASTS

Colour casts are common with night shots, as there is a multitude of different artificial lights. Although these can be corrected by camera filtration, it is easier to use Adobe Elements. On the whole most shots won't need correcting, as it is this very mix of colour that adds to the flavour of the shot.

EXPERIMENTING

Try photographing urban neon signs with a zoom burst. This creates wonderful streaks of coloured light radiating out from the centre. An exposure greater than five seconds will work – too short and you won't have time to finish zooming. This is a somewhat hit-and-miss affair so take lots of shots with different shutter speeds and vary the zoom.

The traffic trails (top) were deliberately included to add to the drama of the shot. They also helped to hide an otherwise boring road.

Get up high (centre) for a great shot. Look out for buildings with public access.

This started life as a day-time shot (below). Altering the contrast and colour and adding a moon turned it into a pseudo-Hollywood image. In the cinema a dark blue filter was traditionally used to simulate night.

FACT FILE

Photographing by moonlight

Photographing the moon is a challenge. Shooting during a full moon will increase your chances, but good shots are possible with the moon in all its different phases. The main problem is that the moon overexposes very quickly, as it is so bright in comparison to the land. Also, an exposure greater than 10 seconds causes the moon to blur as it moves across the sky. It can be wiser to use an image-editing program to remove the blurred moon and replace it with an image shot separately. Shoot the moon at the longest setting on your lens and use a tripod to maintain maximum sharpness. If your camera has a spot facility, take a reading from the moon and bracket several exposures around it.

Movement and shutter speeds

This close-up detail of a rock in a river was taken with an exposure of 10 seconds in dull lighting conditions. The duller the conditions, the easier it is to produce long exposures without resorting to neutral density filters. You can use the top half of a grey grad as a neutral density filter.

Capturing movement is dependent on aperture size and shutter speed. Don't be put off by the technical aspects of this subtle craft – even a rudimentary understanding of movement will allow you to create breathtaking images.

A photograph can be radically altered by the shutter speed that you choose for capturing the image. Long shutter speeds allow moving elements within the shot to blur for effect, while short, fast shutter speeds allow the subject to be frozen so that more detail can be seen. It depends on the mood and style that you wish to convey to your viewer. Long shutter speeds give a more ethereal mood, while faster shutter speeds allow you to focus on a particular subject, bringing it into sharper focus within the photo. A field of wheat can look soft and sensuous with a long shutter speed, or stark and well-defined with a short shutter speed.

LONG SHUTTER SPEEDS

When I first started to take an interest in photography I remember seeing shots of the sea that looked as though the water had turned to mist. It seemed as though they had been shot on another planet. Of course, I now know that it was merely a special technique that caused the blurring effect.

The effect was created by a simple technique by which you extend the shutter speed, so that the exposure takes full seconds rather than fractions of a second. A tripod, or at least a solid support such as a wall, is vital for long shutter speeds. Without it you will end up with camera shake, which will completely ruin the shot unless the effect is intentional (*see motion blur filter effects on page 82*).

Most of the time, long shutter speeds are easily achieved: you just stop down the lens to produce a sufficiently long exposure. In some circumstances, you may find that the ambient light levels are so bright that slow shutter speeds cannot be achieved, even when the lens is fully stopped down. In this case, a polarizer or neutral grad filter is needed to reduce the light levels for a sufficiently long exposure. Using a filter also allows a larger aperture to be used, giving a narrower depth of field.

FAST SHUTTER SPEEDS

Although slower speeds are the norm for landscape work, you may on occasion need a fast shutter speed to freeze your subject. One particular subject that springs to mind is flowers. I always keep an eye out for detail within the landscape and often it is the colour and beauty of flowers that catches my attention. As flowers will sway even in the lightest breeze, a fast shutter speed becomes essential in order to freeze them in mid-sway. The obvious choice for increasing shutter

Shooting on a dull day without adding any orange warm-up colour correction filters will often result in a very strong blue colour cast. This is perfect for cold wintry shots. A soft-focus filter has softened the image slightly.

speed is to open up your lens aperture. This increases the amount of light getting to the CCD chip, thus allowing a faster shutter speed to be chosen. Naturally, wider apertures mean less depth of field, so there is always an ongoing battle between shutter speed for faster speeds and the aperture for extra depth of field. Often, a compromise has to be sought, but it is useless having good depth of field if the subject matter is blurred due to too long an exposure. In such an event, you have to forget depth of field concerns in order to capture the subject sharply. Thankfully, in many cases – especially with flowers – limited depth of field can actually accentuate the subject. I often try out a number of shutter speeds and see which one gives the best mixture between sharpness and depth of field.

One technique to try is using fill-in flash, which freezes the subject and may allow a longer shutter speed for better depth of field.

I normally shoot when there is a gap in the wind that stops everything from moving, but you can also use the wind to create deliberate blur effects. This works especially well with flowers and crops.

Shot at different shutter speeds (4 secs, 1/2 sec, 1/30 sec), this series of shots shows how the shutter speed affects flowing water during an exposure. Always try various shutter speeds to get a variety of effects.

Lens filters

These two images graphically show the effect of a polarizing filter. In the shot below, the polarizing filter has made the sky much more dramatic. The sky itself is a much deeper blue colour, while the clouds have increased contrast.

Many digital photographers may be surprised by my allegiance to traditional lens filters. True, a lot can be done using the filters in a software package, but some effects are only possible using on-camera filters. These are placed in front of the lens before the shot is taken. A little extra care and the thoughtful use of filters at the shooting stage can save unnecessary corrections later on.

TIP Always shoot with the sun at a 90° angle to your camera for maximum polarization of the light to occur.

POLARIZING FILTER

The polarizing filter is without doubt the most important filter you can use. Its effect is truly magical, and it can transform a picture with a simple twist of the filter.

The polarizing filter polarizes the light that reflects off most non-metallic objects. Light travels in many directions and the polarizer prevents certain wavelengths from passing through to the lens. This reduces glare and haze, which in turn increases the clarity and colour saturation of your shot.

Glare is also eliminated so that shiny surfaces such as windows and water will lose any reflections in them and darken in tone. Beautiful Mediterranean seas will turn transparent, making boats seem as if they are floating in mid-air. The maximum effect occurs when the filter is at a 45° angle to the reflection. These effects are impossible to re-create on the computer.

The biggest drawback with the polarizer is that it reduces the light that reaches your CCD sensor by two stops. In bright conditions this is not a worry, but you will need to use longer exposures and a tripod for lower light levels. Polarizers are made in two types: circular and linear. Both do exactly the same job but are intended to accommodate different designs in camera exposure meters. You may have to do some research to find out which one will work on your camera.

On-camera filters should still be an integral part of your digital camera kit. The polarization of light effect has yet to be turned into a computer plug-in filter.

GREY GRADUATE FILTER

This is a very important filter and should be in your camera bag along with the polarizer. The grey graduate (or grey grad) is primarily used for balancing the light levels of the sky and land. It has a graduated grey neutral-density colour that fades to clear plastic half-way down. Skies are often several f-stops brighter than the land and without filtration you end up with a washed-out sky if you expose for the land, or a dark landscape if you expose for the sky. Smaller cameras may need a special filter holder to use a grey grad correctly.

NEUTRAL-DENSITY FILTER

A neutral-density filter is useful for deliberately reducing the light entering the camera to allow a longer shutter speed to be used. Longer shutter speeds can be used creatively to add motion in water. They are only needed if the light levels are so bright that your smallest aperture is still giving too fast a shutter speed. Try combining a neutral density and polarizer for really long exposures.

ULTRAVIOLET FILTER

This is normally the only screw-on filter that you will need to buy. Its effect is difficult to gauge but it cuts down UV, which can turn images shot in high-altitude places to blue. The filter's main benefit is that it acts as a high-quality protective cover for your expensive lens. A UV filter costs only a fraction of a new front lens element and protects against anything that can ruin a camera lens.

SOFT-FOCUS FILTER

A soft-focus effect can be applied to just about any subject in any lighting with great success. It should not be confused with an out-of-focus image. Although very nice effects can be made with Adobe Photoshop Elements using the *Gaussian Blur* filter, they will not replicate the effect that a soft-focus filter has when placed in front of the lens.

The lens filter creates a radiant glow around the edge of the highlights. It bleeds into the shadows and makes them slightly lighter. This effect is very difficult to achieve on the computer; a low-cost filter can give your shots a different creative avenue to go down. There are hundreds of soft-focus filters available, but you can also easily create your own filter. Use transparent cellophane, plastic self-adhesive tape, nylon stockings or simply breathe on the lens.

When shooting, use a wide aperture, as small apertures will lessen the effect. Also, try overexposing to enhance the glow, and shoot your subject with a dark background so that the edges glow more prominently.

FACT FILE

Filter holders and filter types
Owners of digital SLRs can attach filters as they would to a normal SLR. For other digital camera designs, you may need a specific lens or filter adaptor in order to use them. Filters come in many different designs. Screw-on filters attach directly to your lens and often remain there. Others are small thin rectangular plastic sheets that slide into a special holder, or are held over the lens by hand.

A filter holder attaches to the front of your lens and allows you to slide the filters into place. You can rotate the holder to any angle and position the filter to any given point, making it a very useful piece of kit to have in your camera bag.

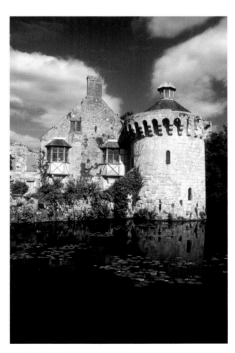

These two shots show the effectiveness of using a grey graduate filter in front of the lens. Some people argue that corrections to density can be done later on, but if shadow detail isn't picked up by the original camera exposure, then this becomes impossible.

Weather

MIST AND FOG

One of the most interesting weather conditions that you can experience is mist or fog. Most of us wouldn't dream of venturing out on cold, wet, misty days, but you are depriving yourself of one of nature's most ethereal and magical weather conditions. Adverse weather conditions often produce far more interesting shots than those achieved on sunny days with a bland blue sky and featureless light.

Sometimes, if you get up early enough, you will witness mist forming in the valley bottoms or on lakes. If the sun happens to shine, the resulting interplay of light and vapour can produce beautiful

O ne of the biggest obstacles a photographer has to overcome is the weather. If luck is on your side, the weather can provide drama and atmosphere by the bucketful. If you get no luck, however, then you may be packing your bags and going home early. The weather has the potential to be your greatest friend or worst enemy. It is the one underlying ingredient that binds the whole image together to bring success or failure.

TIP Always hang around if the weather takes a turn for the worst. Your perseverance is often rewarded with atmospheric and moody shots.

Dawn is often a good time to find mist, as the cold air has settled on the ground during the night. This was shot with a telephoto lens to emphasize one foreground tree

against the misty background. Mist and fog can produce some great backdrops, which allow you to place greater emphasis on your subject.

It had started off sunny the day this shot was taken, but then a sea mist suddenly rolled up out of nowhere. Most people pack up their bags and leave in these conditions,

but I stayed on to get some really atmospheric and unusual shots showing the pier shrouded in mist.

With the right clothing a photographer should be able, ready and willing to tackle any weather conditions. Often the harsher the weather, the greater and more dramatic the photographic opportunity on offer.

 Photographed on a dull day, this shot has isolated a small detail from the forest. Take advantage of the telephoto end of the lens to get rid of sky if it's not very interesting. Although shot in colour, this is almost a monochromatic image – if it weren't for the hint of red bark on the trees.

Hoar frost is an amazing sight, turning even the tiniest details into ice as if someone has sprayed the trees with white paint. These conditions usually give you a beautiful electric-blue sky the next day, so the contrast between the sky and the trees is excellent. Try a polarizer, but remember to compensate with two extra stops during exposure. To maintain sharpness, I always increase the shutter speed rather than open the aperture.

shots. You have to get there early, as the mist will quickly evaporate when the sun warms up. On duller days the mist can hang around for much longer, allowing you to be more relaxed about photo opportunities.

Mist and fog do a fantastic job of creating instantaneous depth in a photograph. Foreground objects usually loom out of the mist, isolated from background detail by the fog. Try to get in close to a subject so that it dominates the shot and faint detail can be seen in the background. Many places that do not usually offer much photogenic potential in normal weather conditions can spring to life when background clutter is hidden.

I had just driven through a storm when the sun suddenly appeared at the storm's edge. A lone tree in a stark, wild landscape with a stormy sky and great side lighting. It doesn't get much more dramatic than this!

RAIN, STORMS, RAINBOWS

Really rough weather can produce some of my favourite photographic conditions. There are few sights more dramatic than the sun breaking out from behind a storm cloud to illuminate the land with beautiful shafts of light. Great shots are to be had almost anywhere in the urban environment as well as the rural one. You can never tell when such conditions are going to happen, so you need to be on your guard to capture them. Usually you will be out and about doing mundane chores and suddenly the heavens will open up to reveal a fantastic photo opportunity. You must carry your camera with you at all times in order to capture these moments. One such incident occurred on my way to a haircut whilst living in Spain. The sun popped out and lit the road and lighthouse in spectacular fashion, adding a stormy steel-grey sky for maximum impact. No camera, no shot. So remember the golden rule.

Four seasons

Spring and summer offer green trees and warm weather for shooting in. Make the most of this with walks in areas of natural beauty.

In autumn you have to keep a careful eye on the colour of the trees as they turn golden. Definitely worth booking a week off work for this!

SPRING

The time of rebirth and new growth after the long, cold hard winter, spring can be a slow transition from short, dark days to lighter, longer ones. The exuberance of colour, with new flowers and trees blossoming, is a welcome change. The colour of the trees becomes a vivid, intense green, which looks amazing when polarized. Sudden storm showers can add to the drama of spring. Brilliant sunshine, mingling with dark, foreboding storm clouds creates powerful, dramatic picture opportunities.

The yearly weather cycle is split into the classic four seasons of spring, summer, autumn and winter, and each has its own distintive merits and strengths. Learn to take advantage of the best that each season has to offer and take stunning photographs all year round.

TIP Snow is very bright and will fool your exposure meter into underexposing, turning snow grey. Take a reading from the snow and increase the exposure by 1 to 1½ stops as a starting point.

Each season offers a new palette of colours, textures and effects in the landscape for the photographer to get creative with. Enjoy the advantages of each one as the seasons follow each other during the year.

As the sun is still low in the sky, strong side lighting is possible all day; this is ideal for bringing out the shape and texture of the land. Woodlands are a popular haunt for photographers. Often, a slightly overcast day helps when photographing flowers – too much sunlight can cause major contrast problems, ruining any subtle colour details.

Mist is a by-product of cold winter nights, bringing dewdrops glistening like diamonds in the sun. It diffuses the landscape, isolating elements. The colder spring weather is sharp, perfect for crystal-clear panoramic landscapes.

The change from summer to winter in the landscape can be dramatic. Why not try photographing one subject as it changes through the seasons as a project?

SUMMER

The splendour of spring calms down and more rustic colours dominate as the ripening green crops turn golden yellow. Trees fill out and become dark green. The sun is high in the sky for most of the day, creating few shadows. Fields are harvested and giant hay bales adorn the hills, creating strong graphic shapes.

Summer is the most popular time to shoot landscapes, although you will have to wait until late afternoon or get up ludicrously early to capture the light at its finest.

AUTUMN

Without doubt, the photographer's busiest time of year – Mother Nature's gift before the gloom of winter. The glory of colour goes into overdrive, and so will your camera! Keep an eye on the leaves' stage of transition. Autumn can be finished in the space of one or two weekends while you are looking the other way. One bad storm and the wind could destroy all your potential masterpieces overnight.

The golden leaves become more transparent during autumn; and backlighting them can produce stunning results. Try moving in closer to capture the texture of the glowing foliage. Dull days can be good for capturing subtle detail on wider shots – a quick tweak of the *Colour Saturation Hue* tool in Adobe Photoshop Elements will cure any insipid colour problems.

If your camera lens has this facility, try moving in close for a shot of leaves on the ground. A small gold or silver reflector kept in the camera bag can add a touch of fill-in that helps to bring a picture to life. Hold the reflector at an angle to the sun and play around until the reflected light of the sun hits your chosen subject. A sturdy support is necessary as small apertures are needed to retain detail.

WINTER

I cannot wait for the challenge of winter. With the right weather conditions – and there are so many to choose from – magnificent shots are yours for the taking. However, winter is both a giver and a taker. I've lost count of the number of trips ruined by uninspiring weather.

On the other hand, crisp, clear blue skies and plenty of snow falling the night before are heaven-sent conditions for picture-postcard photography. Snow has the amazing effect of hiding everything that is ugly; even the most mundane of places can be transformed into a winter wonderland.

Get up early! Being the first person to tread footsteps onto new virgin snow in the early hours is a fantastic experience. As the sun climbs, shadows remain blue while highlights take on a fiery red colour. This doesn't last for long, but the rest of the day still remains full of photographic opportunities.

Hoar frost has to be the most spectacular show-off of all. It coats trees and all around into a fairytale grotto of the finest ice. Detail shots look amazing if you are lucky enough to find such conditions.

Shooting for post-production

TAKING GREAT LANDSCAPE SHOTS

The boat, sea, moon and sky in this picture were all taken from different shots. (See page 116 for more details of how I created the end result.) Organisation is crucial here. All my CDs have a printout of the contents visible for easy research. Mac users should open the CD, then select Print *from the* File *menu. cut out the list and place it in the front of the CD case.*

You may also try shooting the scene when it is sunny and again when it is cloudy. Some shadow areas will turn pitch black when the sun comes out. Shooting the same scene when the sun goes behind a cloud will reveal detail in the shadows that can then be added to the sunny shot. This gives you the very best of both worlds.

Another interesting technique is to montage several shots together of the same scene, but taken at different times of the day. So the shot call go from day to evening, with several transitions in between.

Remember that a tripod is an absolute necessity for these techniques, as the shots have to be taken from exactly the same position. Small differences in size, angle and composition can be overcome, but will add unnecessary retouching time later on. Larger variations will make the shots look strange due to too much perspective distortion. If a tripod isn't available, an alternative form of support must be found. If all the shots are taken on a tripod and at exactly the same resolution, then they can be put in layers and easily manipulated, as the layers will overlay each other perfectly.

There are times when, for some reason, your shots don't come out right. Exposure is one key area where problems can occur – even when care is taken over meter readings. In tricky lighting conditions, always bracket your shots so that you have a good choice of highlight and shadow detail.

In some cases, clever thinking can save a lot of retouching time later on. Shooting buildings or even remote landscapes can leave the most patient photographer pulling their hair out if a coach party full of snap-happy tourists has just arrived before them. Where you have a lot of people in shot, try shooting the scene at timed intervals. This will allow you to choose a section of the scene from one shot where the people have moved on and paste it into another where you have the least number of people in shot.

TIP For quick access to your material, create folders in your library for each of the topics you may need, such as sky shots, trees, boats, water, sunsets and so on.

Shoot something new every day and build up a digital library of shots that can then be used in montages.

COMBINING SHOTS

Four shots were used to create the final version of this forest scene. The correct exposure suffered from too dark a foreground and the leaves were overexposed in parts of the centre. The foreground from the lighter version was selected with the *Lasso* tool, feathered by 15 pixels and pasted into a new layer. Colour and density were altered to match. The central area of leaves was selected from the darker version, feathered by 100 pixels for a really soft edge and pasted into a new layer.

The majority of this shot was too dark to be of any use, but the leaves in the centre had more contrast and colour to offer.

The overexposed shot has more foreground detail, so I selected that for the composite image.

The relevent parts of all three shots were placed on separate layers (see p68) and combined into this final image.

The correct exposure is too dark in the foreground and too light in the canopy.

This type of shot relies on precise registration. This requires a tripod, so that the image does not move between exposures. It becomes much harder trying to align several shots if they are all taken at slightly different angles. The end result has an evenly balanced and pleasing tone, which is very difficult to achieve in one shot under such contrasting and difficult lighting conditions.

3 Digital darkroom techniques

The abilities of the digital camera are only part of what makes digital photography so satisfying. The other part is image-editing software: the digital equivalent of the photographer's darkroom. Using this software, you can avoid poor colour or wrong exposure, and take advantage of the whole artistic process for yourself. If a shot needs a new sky or a new point of interest, you can put one in. We can have as much control over our shots as painters have had over their paintings for centuries.

Image-editing software

For the digital photographer there is a confusing array of software packages on the market at different prices and skill levels. Many are good, but for this book we're going to stick with one: Adobe Photoshop Elements. Adobe has long been the leader in image-manipulation software with Adobe Photoshop. With the growth of digital photography, Adobe saw the demand for a cheaper, cut-down version of its professional package, and came up with a Photoshop Elements.

Elements retains a range of powerful tools, but does not possess some of Photoshop's professional capabilities, such as complex colour management or CMYK conversions. This is not important because such tools are only really required in professional publishing. For straight photo-manipulation, Elements does everything you need.

LEARN ABOUT LAYERS

In most respects, Elements allows you to do the same things you can do in a photographic darkroom: adjust colour and exposure, crop and straighten, dodge and burn and enlarge. However, Elements has a couple of new tricks for you. The feature you will keep coming back to is *Layers*. This operates like layers of transparent material that you place on top of your photo. You can select and copy elements from your photo, or from other shots, and place these on their own layer so that you can move them around and work on them independently. You can control how transparent these layers are using the *Opacity* control, and how they interact with each other using blend modes. Understanding layers will become a crucial part of your technique.

WORKING WITH AN IMAGE

1 First, import an image into Elements via a film or flatbed scanner, digital camera or photo CD. This is generally done using *File > Open* or by *File > Browse*. This will take you to any files saved on your computer or to the desktop to open a CD. *File > Import* is used for creating a film/flatbed scan via the Twain device. Most cameras come with special software to download the images onto your computer.

2 The first thing to do is save the image. Go *File > Save As* and create a name for the file. Save the file as a Photoshop (PSD) file.

3 Next create a new copy layer. Use *Layer > Duplicate Layer* or, in the *Layers* palette, drag the background layer over to the *New Layer* icon at the bottom (the curled page in the middle of the three icons). This allows you to keep the original background layer intact, so that if you have any catastrophes you still have the original layer to work on. Always create a duplicate layer!

This wide-angle shot was actually created from several different pictures, montages together in Photoshop Elements. This is only the beginning of what you can do in your software.

4 Make general tonal and colour adjustments using the *Levels* command (*see page 88*). At this stage, if you are happy with the result you may duplicate this layer and throw away the original background layer.

5 Make selective local adjustments to colour and tone using the selection tools: the *Rectangular Marquee*, *Lasso* tool, *Magic Wand* and others.

6 Remove any unsightly blemishes from your shot using the *Clone Stamp* tool (*see page 79*).

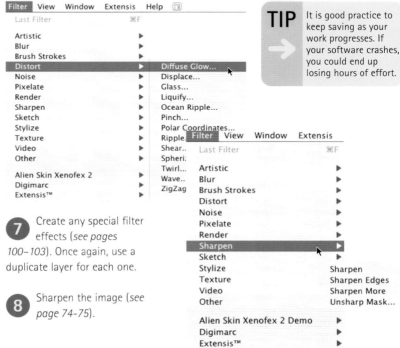

TIP It is good practice to keep saving as your work progresses. If your software crashes, you could end up losing hours of effort.

7 Create any special filter effects (*see pages 100–103*). Once again, use a duplicate layer for each one.

8 Sharpen the image (*see page 74–75*).

9 Next you should resize and crop the image (*see pages 70–71*). This can be done at an earlier stage if you know exactly what the final use of the image is for.

10 Now save the image. Use *File > Save* to keep the file name and format the same. Use *File > Save As* if you want to re-name the file or change the file format from, say, a Photoshop PSD file to a Web-friendly JPEG file format.

Cropping

In this case the Spanish landscape shot was given a completely different feel by cropping out unwanted sky and land. Cropping can be used to make effective panoramic style formats.

Cropping helps to bring order to a shot from a potentially confusing scene. The secret to good cropping is placing the objects within the frame to complement and enhance the main subject. Getting it right isn't always easy *in situ*, although with a bit of practice a zoom lens should allow you to fine-tune your compositions to a precise degree. Even bad shots can be rescued, thanks to the imaging power of your computer.

In the first crop I attempted to place emphasis on the sky. It may have been a good crop to choose for an image with a more dramatic sky with a bold silhouetted foreground, but here it didn't feel right.

Cropping an image is an easy way to improve a photograph. Most diehard photographers will argue that it should always be done in-camera, but I believe that a bit of a 'tuck and snip' later on does no harm. None of us is perfect or so quick as to capture a scene flawlessly every time. A hastily taken shot with a wonky horizon is an easily forgivable offence. You may even have a fixed focal-length lens on your camera, so zooming to crop unwanted detail is not an option. If you can't get in as close as you want, due to a fixed lens or a small telephoto range on your zoom, walk up as close as you can to the subject and crop the rest off later.

I liked the second crop, but it didn't show the ruined farmhouse, which is what initially drew me to the shot in the first place.

This scene was shot both vertically (portrait) and horizontally (landscape). In my opinion, both shots work equally well. The final destination and usage of the image (card, framed print, website or portfolio) may determine which one to use.

 For the final crop I simply added the farm to the bottom of the second shot.

Even with careful composition, you will sometimes change your mind after looking at the shot on-screen. You may just need to remove a sliver at the top or bottom of the image, but more severe cropping is also possible on the computer – though it is best to try and zoom in as much as possible *in situ* because quality can suffer from extreme enlargement of the centre of a photo.

Cropping in Photoshop Elements is easy. Choose the *Crop* tool from the *Tool* menu and the cursor changes. Click where you want the top right of the crop to be, then drag the crop marquee down and to the right. Release the button and a bounding box appears. Drag the top, bottom and side handles to expand the crop, click and hold inside the marquee to drag it around. If you double click inside it the shot will be cropped.

TIP → You can alter the shield colour and its *Opacity* in the *Options Bar* at the top. I use a black colour and an *Opacity* of 80–100% for most work. Click on the colour to change it.

FACT FILE

Achieving different effects

This shot really shows how two different interpretations can be achieved from one image. The original was shot at maximum telephoto length to zoom in on the pier and sun. A telephoto has helped to compress the elements and make the sun bigger in the background. A soft-focus filter was also used in front of the lens. Cropping in to isolate the top of the pier has produced a beautiful yet simple image. The silhouetted shapes add graphic impact to the shot. This would make a great art poster for the wall. Adding a grain filter effect in Elements will add atmosphere.

The original version, shot at around 300mm. Long telephoto shots increase the size of the sun or moon for a dramatic mood.

After cropping, remember to save the file under a different name using the Save As command.

Rotation and straightening

Shot with a focal length of about 100mm after a wedding feast. I can't think why this glorious sunset ended up askew!

The finished version has had its wonky horizon and disappointing colour corrected.

A dobe Photoshop Elements allows you to manually or automatically straighten skewed horizons and also to rotate or flip an image. Rotating images gives you greater flexibility when creating image montages. It allows you to precisely rotate a small element in a layer so that correct perspective is maintained throughout the whole image.

STRAIGHTENING AN IMAGE

A skewed horizon can be very annoying, especially if it is a seascape, where an uneven horizon sticks out like a sore thumb. You will need to rotate the entire image. If you scan using a film or flatbed scanner, the effect can also come about as a result of poorly aligned pictures. Try to be as careful as possible when loading film or prints to be scanned. With prints, you can use the edge of the scanner to butt up against the print to ensure straight edges.

Elements lets you apply perspective; it can also *Scale*, *Rotate*, *Distort* and correct skewed images. The image must be placed on a layer to allow the transformation to be made.

MANUALLY ROTATING A SKEWED HORIZON

1 Because I did not use a tripod for this shot, the original photograph was not horizontal. So I decided to rotate the shot manually.

2 I used *Image* > *Rotate* > *Free Rotate Layer*, which creates a new layer to rotate the image.

For the experienced photographer, minor tweaking is often all that is necessary. Adobe Elements handles such chores easily and quickly.

TIP

It's worth remembering some cheaper zoom lenses can have barrel distortion, which may give a straight horizon a curved appearance. This is the fault of the lens, and not you!

3 When you do this, a bounding box appears around the new layer, with a series of handles attached – you use the corner handle to slowly rotate the image left or right.

5 It is possible to rotate by eye or switch a grid on (*View > Grid*), allowing you to precisely align any line within the image. Go to *Preferences* to alter the colour of the grid and the number of squares.

7 This tool has the familiar handles in each corner and on the sides. Simply drag each side handle outwards and it will stretch the image. Stop when the clear area is covered and repeat for each individual side.

4 In order to straighten the horizon, I rotated the picture to the left. I used the mouse to grab the top left handle and gently rotated by dragging the mouse.

Image	Enhance	Lay
Duplicate Image...		
Rotate	▶	
Transform	▶	**Free Transform** ⌘T
Crop		Skew
Resize	▶	Distort
Adjustments	▶	Perspective
Histogram...		
Mode	▶	

6 When the rotation has finished rotating, it will still leave clear areas that need to be cleaned up. As this was a simple image with large areas of even tone, I got away with using the *Free Transform* tool *(Image > Transform > Free Transform)*.

8 For the bottom of the image I used the *Magic Wand* tool to select the dark sand, then added the clear area by holding down the shift key and reusing the *Magic Wand*. I then used the *Eyedropper* tool to pick up the dark sand colour and fill the selected area.

FACT FILE

Auto-rotate
Sometimes your image may need reversing or turning through 180° in order to correct it. Simply choose *Image > Rotate* and then use any of the submenu commands. Most of the common ones are there, but it also has a *Custom Rotate* to allow for personal fine-tuning.

You can also automatically straighten a skewed horizon by using the *Straighten Image* command *(Image > Rotate > Straighten Image)*. As it relies on Photoshop deducing where the horizon is, this method is a bit more hit-and-miss than the manual method above. Adobe's suggestion of creating a larger canvas size first does seem to improve your chances.

Sharpening

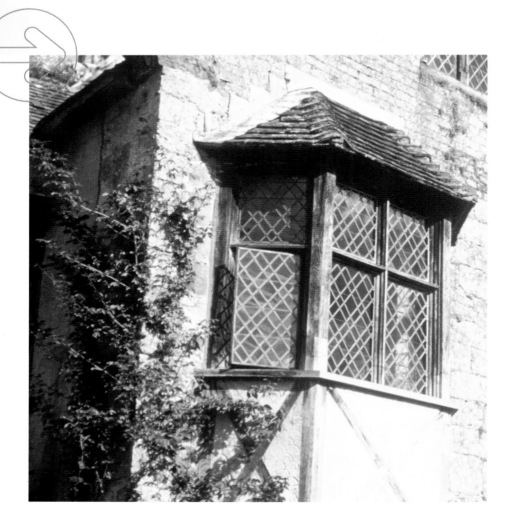

This detail of a shot of an English country house has been blown up to demonstrate the use of the Unsharp Mask.

Sharpening is usually necessary on most photographs, especially if the original has been scanned. You can also improve sharpness if you've not quite focused correctly in the first place, but it won't rescue a disaster, I'm afraid. There are various ways of sharpening in Photoshop Elements, including options in the *Quick Fix* dialog. The range of sharpening filters in the *Filter* menu is, however, much better and much more flexible.

There are several filters to choose from under the *Filter > Sharpen* menu, but most only allow one specific effect which you can't alter. The *Unsharp Mask* filter is the big daddy here – in effect, it is a combination of all the program's *Sharpen* filters. It also has the greatest control, which is exactly what we want. *Unsharp Mask* is based on a traditional method used for sharpening an image where an extra out-of-focus film was exposed with the original to give an apparent increase in sharpness.

USING THE UNSHARP MASK

There are three sliders that control the final effect. Sharpening should be done at the end of the image-manipulation process. Sharpening and then applying further filters or modifications can create unwanted contrast and colour. Sharpening changes the edges of pixels by altering their contrast; further alteration will accentuate this edge contrast. Unsharp masking will also sharpen areas such as skies, which may be better left soft; with this in mind, I normally create a feathered selection around the areas to be sharpened. Unsharp masking also enhances noise and grain, so that shadow areas, which have been brightened, tend to look a little strange. Often, it is advisable to have a duplicate layer so that soft areas can be reintroduced to the sharpened version or vice versa.

This filter effect is more pronounced on-screen than it is in print because the screen is lower in resolution. You would be wise to print out various test settings as a record. Higher-resolution images sharpen much better because the effect on each pixel is much smaller in print than on a low-resolution file.

AMOUNT

The *Amount* slider goes up to 500%. Adobe recommends 150% to 200%, which works well, but I sometimes prefer a higher setting – even all the way up to 500%. The secret is to balance all three sliders to find your own settings.

RADIUS

This controls the width or halo surrounding each pixel when sharpened. Start with a setting between 1.0 and 2.5.

THRESHOLD

This controls which pixels will be affected by the filter. The lower the setting, the more pixels get sharpened. A *Threshold* of 10 to 30 should leave skies relatively unaffected.

Sharpening is often essential, especially for larger prints. But this series of images shows that you can also sharpen an image too much.

1 Amount 200, Radius 2.5, Threshold 8

2 Amount 500, Radius 1.0, Threshold 8

3 Amount 500, Radius 1.4, Threshold 30

Unsharp Mask

OK
Cancel
☑ Preview

100%

Amount: 200 %

Radius: 2.5 pixels

Threshold: 8.0 levels

Unsharp Mask

OK
Cancel
☑ Preview

100%

Amount: 500 %

Radius: 1.0 pixels

Threshold: 8 levels

Unsharp Mask

OK
Cancel
☑ Preview

100%

Amount: 500 %

Radius: 1.4 pixels

Threshold: 30 levels

4 Amount 500, Radius 6.1, Threshold 0

Unsharp Mask

OK
Cancel
☑ Preview

100%

Amount: 500 %

Radius: 6 pixels

Threshold: 1 levels

This sequence shows how the different Unsharp Mask settings affect an image. Various settings were used. The 200/2.5/8 setting looks the most favourable under close scrutiny, but each setting looks fine in isolation. The higher the Amount set, the lower the Radius and the higher the Threshold should be.

Dust and scratches

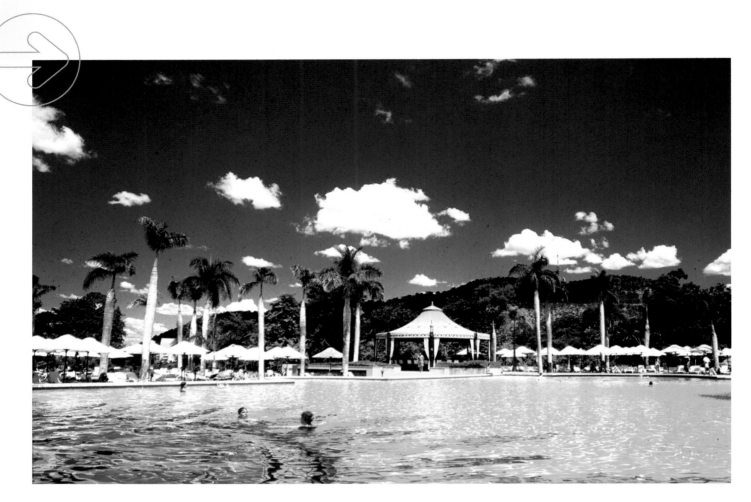

Dust and scratches are a common problem. Older film and flatbed scanners are notorious for picking up every detail on the film or print surface – even after scrupulous cleaning – but even digital cameras can have dust problems. Digital SLR cameras with interchangeable lenses are especially prone to dust, which can lodge on the CCD sensor. Care should be taken to avoid this problem by carefully cleaning the CCD with a blower brush on a regular basis.

An old holiday snap that was scanned in using a flatbed scanner. Time has not treated the original slide very well and it is in a poor state of repair. After scanning, the snap needs to undergo a complete overhaul.

Although time-consuming, a routine can be created to quickly sort out these problems. For photos where lots of dust speckles are present, the quickest option is to use the *Dust and Scratches* filter in Photoshop Elements. You may be tempted to just run the filter over the entire image, but this will result in a universal distortion (it does, in fact, produce a nice watercolour effect that you can deliberately try out on the entire image if you wish to experiment).

PRECISION REMOVAL

Most dust and scratches require a fairly powerful effect to remove them. Each imperfection, therefore, needs to be selected individually using the *Lasso* tool. By narrowing the selection to a small area around each bit of dust, the filter effect is localized and minimized. The secret is to select a dozen or so areas at a time. Use the shift key to add extra selections to the original one and then apply the filter. Using this method you will soon finish the entire picture area.

You no longer have to live with prints that are ruined by specks of dust or scratches just because a photo lab didn't clean your negatives properly before printing. With patience and application you can remove them from the image.

1 At first glance it's difficult to see any sign of dust on this digital image, but look closer and you can see the marks breaking up the blue of the sky. Here, numerous flecks of dust have been selected using the *Lasso* tool. Hold down the Shift key to keep adding to the selection. Try to follow the shape and size of each bit of dust as you select it.

2 The *Dust and Scratches* dialog box has two sliders. The first slider sets the pixel radius. This instructs the software how many pixels to change within your selection. *Threshold* allows you to alter the severity of the change. Use the preview box to fine-tune these settings. Start the *Radius* at 2 and increase it until all the dust disappears, then increase the *Threshold* from zero and stop when the right level of grain appears. If the *Threshold* is left on zero you will get smooth spots, which will give the game away. Keep the area selected, but use the *Grain* filter with a low-value setting to even out the tone.

3 Some larger flecks of dust may need several passes of the filter. Deselect and reselect the larger spots only. It may be necessary to use the *Clone Stamp* tool (see page 79) on really stubborn flecks of dust.

TIP The *Dust and Scratches* filter smoothes out the surrounding tone, which can leave traces. To cover this, use the *Add Noise* filter with a low *Amount* setting to add texture back in.

Removing unwanted picture elements

Nowadays, the digital photographer is also the digital surgeon: able to cut, copy and reposition any part of an image to his or her satisfaction. Principal among the many tools available is the Clone Stamp tool: this enables you to resample any part of an image and remove any details you are unhappy with. In the fight against ugly objects, it is a formidable weapon.

There are two forms of unwanted elements: those that are within your control and those that are not. For those instances that are within your control, the classic example is that of shooting someone with a pole sticking out of their head, and landscapes are no exception to this problem. Such intrusions spoil the flow of the eye around the shot and are easily avoided witha little time and effort and a slight change of viewpoint.

Sometimes, though, you will find that things are beyond your control. Lamp posts, aerials, traffic signs or telegraph poles are just a few of the immovable problems you can encounter on your travels.

Fortunately, whatever the problem, Adobe Photoshop Elements allows you to remove these irritations effortlessly, and transform the scene as if by magic. For me, this is one of the most important tools any software package can offer.

Many of my shots don't need major changes – I simply tweak the exposure and colour. TV aerials and litter are, however, two of my biggest personal bugbears. The ability to remove unwanted elements from a shot allows you to shoot subjects that, prior to the advent of digital, were a waste of film and money, or which would have needed expensive professional retouching.

Retouching can be a complicated process. This shot needed to have several techniques applied to it in order to fix all the problems.

COPYING AND GRAFTING

On this shot, the first step involves selecting and copying an area of even tone to cover over a telegraph wire that runs across the sky. In areas of flat colour, where there isn't much detail to give the game away, this can be the most effective method of hiding something that spoils the picture.

Navigator   More ▶

100%

1 One efficient way of mending photographs is to use the *Lasso* tool to graft a good bit of photograph over the offending area. In this example, it is far quicker to select and copy an area just above the telegraph wire using the *Polygonal Lasso* tool (which is useful for straight lines) than it would be to use the *Clone Stamp* tool to paint over it.

Feather Selection

Feather Radius: 6   pixels

OK
Cancel
Help

3 Now press Command + C on the Mac keyboard (or Ctrl + C for Windows) and then Command + V (Ctrl + V) and the selection will be copied to a new layer. Use the *Move* tool to place the new area over the damaged area. You can move the selection without putting it onto a new layer, but you won't be able to make any changes to it later, such as altering the tone or colour, or using the eraser to remove small areas that should not be there.

2 Make the selection, then choose *Select > Feather* to feather it by 6 pixels. With such thin, small selections you have to use a very small pixel number or your selection won't have any information left in it. But if you don't feather, the selection will have very hard edges that will stand out a mile. Try feathering between 2 and 9 pixels.

Removing unwanted picture elements

CLONING, MOVING AND GRAFTING

Difficult and complicated areas in the photograph will require the use of several tools and techniques. You will need to master them all before you can achieve the clean result you want.

1 In this example I have used the *Dust and Scratches* filter, the *Clone* tool, grafting technique and the *Paintbrush* to correct an awful mess.

2 Here the small dust has been selected so that I can use the *Dust and Scratches* filter. See page 77 for more details of this technique.

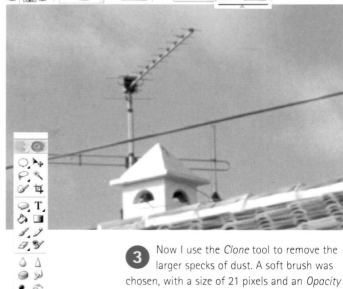

3 Now I use the *Clone* tool to remove the larger specks of dust. A soft brush was chosen, with a size of 21 pixels and an *Opacity* of 50%. A lower *Opacity* allows tricky areas to be cleaned up gradually. Starting with a high *Opacity* and lowering it as you keep working on the same area will give a much smoother tonal finish to the job.

DIGITAL DARKROOM TECHNIQUES

Successful retouching is all about attention to detail. Use tools with small brush sizes and at low *Opacity* settings in complicated areas. Patience is definitely a virtue here.

TIP When using the *Clone* tool, tick the *Aligned* box so that you can resample as you go along. Alt-click at regular intervals to change the sample point.

6 I then use the *Clone* tool to remove the remaining bits of aerial. When cloning close to another boundary, you should make a selection to avoid cloning over the wrong area. In this case, I selected the white chimney and inverted the selection. It was then safe to clone right up to the chimney without affecting it.

4 I now use the grafting technique to remove the aerial, as it is quite a large area to clone. Carefully select around the aerial, *Feather* by 3 pixels and then move the selection to a clean bit of sky nearby. Do not use the *Move* tool – keep the *Lasso* tool icon selected in the tool menu or you will move the aerial itself. As before, copy the sky area to a new layer over the aerial.

7 The other half of the aerial is selected with the *Polygonal Lasso* tool and the area is then cloned.

5 The same grafting technique is used to remove the wire.

8 I use the *Eyedropper* tool to select the white colour of the chimney and then the *Paint Brush* tool, set to maximum 100% *Opacity*, to paint over the remaining bit of the aerial.

Soft-focus and motion blur

The Luminosity blend mode uses hue and saturation from the base layer and the luminance of the blend layer. It gives a lovely glowing effect similar to using a soft-focus filter on the camera lens.

This original shot was given several variations in Photoshop, using a Gaussian Blur *filter* with a Radius *of 5 and blend modes.*

With the Darken blend mode applied, this looks like an airbrushed image with a fine black-and-white mask placed over it.

Using blend modes allows you to create some exciting and interesting effects that are not possible in-camera. It is important to grasp that you need two or more layers of the same image for the blend mode to work. In fact, you can create many layers, one on top of the other, and play about with the blend options. The layer above interacts with the layer below. You can also give one of the layers a filter effect like *Gaussian Blur* or *Watercolour.*

Combining effects filters with blend modes can produce some interesting and artistic images. You can find the blend mode menu in the *Layers* palette, and it has 24 different options available. In the simplest terms, the blend mode establishes how the pixels in one layer will interact with those in the layer below it. As a result, you cannot set a blend mode for the background layer, as it doesn't have any layers below it. Try experimenting – it's always worth clicking from one blend mode to the next to see what the result will look like.

In these examples, we combine blend modes with the *Gaussian Blur* and *Motion Blur* filters. You can easily see how the different blend modes affect each image.

TIP Experiment with blend modes by creating duplicate layers and applying different blend modes to each. Switch layer visibility on and off, watching for useful combinations.

The *Gaussian Blur* filter (*Filter > Blur > Gaussian Blur*) adds extra mood to this pier shot. If you are looking for a softened effect, it is the perfect partner for using with *Blend* modes.

Blending layers

By experimenting with blend modes you can create some beautiful colour effects, as you can see from this example. Run through the options in the *Layers* palette's pop-out menu. Be warned – experimenting with effects is addictive!

For this image, the background layer was copied and blurred using the Gaussian Blur *filter.*

I then chose Pin Light *blend mode and a 61%* Opacity *to reduce the effect. I copied this layer again and this time I chose* Saturation *blend mode and an* Opacity *of 100%.*

This is a combination of the Darken *and* Luminosity *blend modes. A* Luminosity *layer above the* Darken *layer puts back the highlights that the* Darken *blend mode removes, giving you the best of both worlds.*

I created five layers all using the Luminosity *blend mode and flattened them. A lot of fine detail was destroyed, but it created a soft dreamy image that I rather like.*

Soft-focus and motion blur

1 For these images, the main sunflower was carefully selected using the *Magic Wand* and *Lasso* selection tools. The selection was saved and feathered by 2 pixels, and the sunflower remained selected for all the blur effects. This group of images demonstrates how the action of feathering your selection softens the pixels to produce a smooth mask edge.

2 Below, I used an *Angle* of 45° to create a diagonal blur effect to add tension to the image. The *Distance* was set to 355 pixels to give a moderately strong result.

The *Motion Blur* effect and landscape photography might seem like an incongruous pairing, but in fact the *Motion Blur* filters can add a softening, impressionistic, or even dynamic quality to the subject matter. In these examples I've used the *Motion Blur* and its close cousin the *Radial Blur* – in both *Radial* and *Zoom* mode.

Use the *Motion Blur* filter on colourful images to create beautiful abstracts like these. Strong, geometric shapes like trees work really well.

Radial Blur
Amount   12
Blur Center
Blur Method:
● Spin
○ Zoom
Quality:
○ Draft
● Good
○ Best
OK
Cancel

3 For this example, I applied the *Radial Blur* effect to the same image. The blur was moved slightly off-centre so that the effect radiated around the main flower. The effect resembles ripples in a pond.

4 This is the sunflower image with the *Radial Blur* effect in *Zoom* mode. The blur centre was again offset slightly.

FACT FILE

Radial Blur
Amount   100
Blur Center
Blur Method:
○ Spin
● Zoom
Quality:
○ Draft
● Good
○ Best
OK
Cancel

Zoom-burst

The daffodils were perfect for applying a *Radial Blur*. First, I created a duplicate layer. It can be found in the *Blur* filter submenu, in which there is a choice of *Spin* or *Zoom*. *Spin* may be used for creating a shot similar to rotating the camera during exposure, while *Zoom* is very similar to an in-camera zoom-burst technique; using a camera you zoom the lens from wide to telephoto during a longish exposure. This creates a zoom-burst effect that is emulated by the *Radial Blur* filter. I used the filter at 100% and chose the *Zoom* blur. Finally, I erased the centre of the daffodils on the *Zoom* blur layer to allow the original distortion-free flowers to come through.

Manipulating colour, contrast and tone

 This image started off looking slightly gloomy, so the task was to inject some more life and colour back in. First of all, I selected the sky so that only its colour would be altered.

TIP → Most color fixes can be made using adjustment layers, which alter colour values without permanantly altering the image. See *Layer > New Adjustment Layer* for the options.

Photoshop Elements has a number of tools at its disposal to allow colours, contrast and tone to be manipulated in several different ways. By using or combining tools such as the *Levels* command, *Color Variations,* the *Color Cast* quick fix and the *Hue/Saturation* dialog, you can sort out overarching colour problems, brighten or subdue particular colours, desaturate all or part of an image, and fix nearly any contrast or exposure problem you may encounter.

COLOUR VARIATIONS

The easiest way to adjust the colour of an image is through the *Colour Variations* tool (*Enhance > Adjust Colors > Color Variations*). This dialog box has several options available. Firstly, select which area of the image you want to adjust; usually the mid-tones will give the strongest overall colour change. Then select the strength of the change using the colour-intensity slider. Set it to a subtle level, towards the left-hand side. You can then keep adding colour and build up the image slowly, unless you are after a deliberately strong effect – in which case, pull the slider to the right. Use the *Multiple Undo* button to step backwards if you take the effect too far. Use the *Reset* button to go back to the beginning.

 I made the sky bluer and lighter, by clicking on *Increase Blue* and then on the *Lighten* button.

There are a number of different ways of changing colour and contrast, depending on what level of skill you want to achieve.

3 I now selected the field, feathering by 35 pixels for a soft transition between the two areas of the image. Without feathering, it would look false, cut-out and obviously manipulated.

4 Launching *Color Variations* again, I added a small amount of red and yellow to warm the colour up. I also moved the intensity slider to the left for a more subtle build-up of colour. With the colours in the land and sky beefed up, the final image now has a lot more punch.

FACT FILE

Colour cast

The *Color Cast* quick-fix tool (*Enhance > Adjust colours > Color Cast*) should be your first choice if you need to fix an overall colour cast. It uses an eyedropper to identify and then neutralize the problem. For the effect to work, you must click on an area that is supposed to be white, neutral grey or black. This late afternoon shot has turned a little green. I chose the *Color Cast* tool to quickly remove the offending colour, having clicked on the white parts of the clouds in the sky to correct the green colour cast. It may take several tries to get the colour you are after. To avoid creating new colour casts, select the problem areas before using the tool.

Manipulating colour

2 Here, the histogram suggested that I should move the right-hand slider to the left to brighten the shot. I also moved the grey slider to the left to brighten the midtones of the picture, and finally I moved the black slider a little to the right to increase contrast slightly in the shadows.

ADJUSTING TONE AND CONTRAST

The *Levels* dialog (*Enhance > Adjust Brightness /Contrast > Levels*) allows you to correct colour balance and tonal values at the same time. It is the most powerful and precise method of adjusting colour and tone.

FIXING CONTRAST/BRIGHTNESS

In the *Levels* dialog, what looks like a mountain range is in fact a histogram of the photograph's pixel tonal range. On the left are the shadows, on the right the highlights and in between all other tones. Underneath the histogram are three sliders: from left to right, the black slider alters shadows, the grey slider alters midtones and the white slider alters highlights. To set the black and white points correctly, simply pull the black slider to the right and the white slider to the left so that they meet the first pixels to appear on the mountain range. This will give the optimum tonal and contrast range for the sampled image. You can, of course, adjust these further to make the picture's contrast darker or lighter. For overall changes to the tonal value use the grey slider. Move it to the right for brighter pictures and to the left for darker ones.

1 The histogram at the top shows that the highlights in this image need brightening. Simply move the white triangle to the right so that it reaches the start of the histogram, as seen in the lower picture.

allows the colour, contrast and brightness all to be tweaked from one dialog box.

4 In this correctly exposed image, the tonal detail is clearly present on the histogram. The numerous peaks are created by the high-contrast image. By moving the highlight slider from 255 to 247 and the shadow slider from 0 to 11 you create an optimized tonal range showing the maximum amount of detail. You could, of course, tweak the midtone slider to make it darker by moving to the left, or brighter by moving to the right.

FACT FILE

Eyedroppers

You can also use the black and white eyedroppers in the bottom right-hand corner to correct the highlight and shadow points in an image, and adjust the threshold values to pinpoint maximum and minimum values (often called Dmax and Dmin). Hold down the Alt key and drag the white or black slider inwards. The posterized threshold image clearly shows where the white and black areas are. Now use the white and black eyedroppers and click in the relevant shadow and highlight areas. This should set the black and white points to give correct tone and colour. When using the white eyedropper do not click on a specular highlight, as this is not a true highlight with detail in it.

3 In this deliberately overexposed shot you can see that the highlight part of the histogram on the right is peaking out of control, showing that there is a serious loss of highlight detail. The rest of the histogram shows very little detail. This is clearly visible in the original image. The opposite would occur to the left part of the histogram if shadow detail was missing. The normal 'mountain range' in the middle is missing, meaning that there is detail not present that cannot be recreated by the computer.

Manipulating colour

1 This example shows exactly what *Levels* can do for your colours. This is the basic shot, without any adjustment to the *Levels*.

TIP Take one image and play around with the slider control in the *Levels* dialog box to get a feel for the way the tool works.

ADVANCED COLOUR CONTROLS

While *Levels* is the ideal tool for adjusting the range of tones or the contrast of an image, it's equally capable when it comes to controlling colour. In the *Channels* pop-up menu of the *Levels* palette, you can select a single colour channel (*Red*, *Blue* or *Green* in the standard RGB mode) and use the sliders to adjust the colour intensity. The grey slider in the *Red* channel turns the picture red when moved to the left and cyan to the right. In the *Green* channel it moves the image towards green when shifted to the left and magenta when moved to the right. The *Blue* channel goes blue to the left and yellow to the right.

Along with the black and white eyedroppers in the bottom right-hand corner, you will find the grey eyedropper, which works in exactly the same way as the *Color Cast* quick-fix tool. Zoom in and try to find a colour that should be grey, click on it, and the image should be colour-corrected. Sometimes you need to hunt around and try several points before finding a true grey. If you use the black and white eyedroppers to correct highlight and shadow points, you may need the grey eyedropper to fix any colour cast that creeps in.

2 First of all, I switched to the *Red* colour channel and moved the grey slider to the left to accentuate the reds.

3 This is the same image, with the *Levels* still working on the *Red* channel. This time, by moving the slider to the right I shifted the image towards cyan.

DIGITAL DARKROOM TECHNIQUES

You can create dramatic or subtle colour shifts using the *Levels* command. Combine it with selections and adjustment layers for complete control over the colours in your image.

Hue/Saturation

The *Hue/Saturation* command (*Enhance > Adjust Colou r> Hue/Saturation*) allows you to alter the colour (the *Hue*), the *Saturation* and the *Lightness* of selected areas or of the entire image.

To alter all colours at once, select *Master* and adjust the *Hue* or *Saturation* using the appropriate slider. Adjusting colours is best done by eye rather than by entering a specific value. The *Hue* slider is only of use if you want to create some bizarre colour shifts. Minor tweaks can improve colours. I mainly use it to alter skies when too much purple has crept into the blue colour. You can click on the *Edit* menu bar and choose a specific colour to alter.

The *Saturation* tool is great for livening up colours, and is ideal for beefing up a blue sky that is a little insipid. Too much saturation, however, can create radical colour shifts.

4 I've now switched to the *Green* colour channel. This time, moving the slider to the left promotes a green colouring. Moving the slider to the right makes the whole image more magenta.

5 In the *Blue* channel, moving the slider to the left accentuates the blue, while moving it to the right pushes the image towards yellow.

Manipulating colour

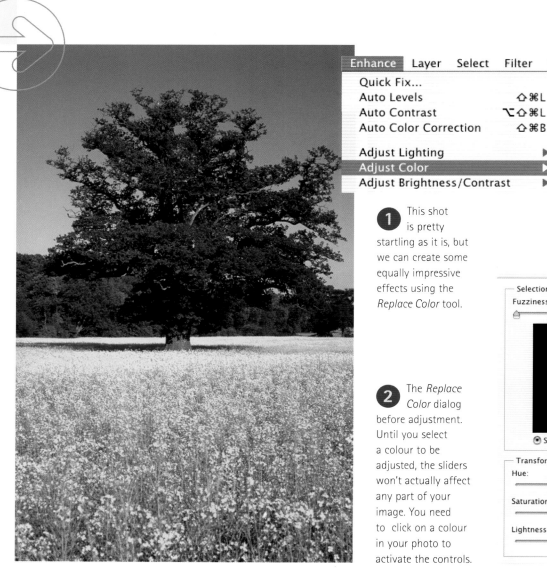

1 This shot is pretty startling as it is, but we can create some equally impressive effects using the *Replace Color* tool.

2 The *Replace Color* dialog before adjustment. Until you select a colour to be adjusted, the sliders won't actually affect any part of your image. You need to click on a colour in your photo to activate the controls.

REMOVING AND REPLACING COLOURS

Two more tools allow quite radical changes to the colouring of your image. The *Remove Color* tool allows you to remove all colour from an image and turn it into a black-and-white image. The advantage is that the image isn't converted to greyscale, but remains an RGB image. This is particularly useful if you want to transform a colour photo into a black-and-white image without risking its levels of tone or contrast *(see page 102)*.

REPLACE COLOUR

Enhance > Adjust Color > Replace Color
The second command is a useful tool for both colour and black-and-white images that you want to tone with a colour. You may, for example, wish to change a specific colour in an image without affecting other colours. When the dialog box opens, you click on the colour you want to change. Use the + eyedropper to add to the selection. It creates a temporary mask that can be altered with the tolerance slider. You can then use the *Hue* slider to change the selected colour. If, for example, the

reds have come out too strong, you can select and alter them. This is very similar to the *Hue/Saturation* tool, with the advantage that you can create your own selection when required. It really comes into its own when colouring black-and-white images.

TIP In images where there is a blue colour in the sky and foreground, try selecting the sky first before opening the *Replace Color* dialog box.

For a more radical colour change I turned the yellow rapeseed to red to create an instant poppy field. Montaging one or two actual poppies into the scene would give it that extra bit of realism.

3 Pull the *Fuzziness* slider to about 100, roughly halfway, and click on a colour to be changed – in this case the blue sky is chosen. Simply click on another colour if you want to change your mind. Look at the *Sample* box to check.

5 Here I have given the sky a lurid pink to illustrate the impact of the colour change. Move the *Hue* slider to +92 to create the colour change. Small clumps of pixels may not have been selected, so use the *Clone Stamp* to fix them afterwards.

4 Click on the + eyedropper to add more blue tonal variations. Once done, use the *Fuzziness* slider to fine-tune the mask. The small image will illustrate the effect of the slider moving, with the white area growing as it moves upwards. The higher the *Fuzziness*, the more blues that are selected.

6 For the final image I wanted a more natural results. I tweaked the blue to +13 on the *Hue* slider, +8 on the *Saturation* and – 4 on the *Lightness* slider. This has very subtly darkened the blue sky, adding tonal depth to the shot.

Replacing a sky

Quite often, the weather can play cruel tricks on us when out and about taking photographs. Whenever you want a blue sky it always seems to cloud over, or you may have the foreground bathed in sun, only for the sky to be insipid and boring. With Adobe Photoshop Elements it is possible to replace the sky with a nice blue one and rescue a shot that would otherwise be destined for the bin.

 This shot has a moody and dramatic sky, but I wanted a give it a calmer, lighter feel.

1 Firstly, you will need to find a blue-sky shot from your files. It is often a good idea to shoot a selection of nice skies to file away for such an emergency. Try to shoot using a similar focal length and avoid foreground clutter.

2 The sky shot and the mountain shot were opened. Both were made small on the screen so they could be viewed side by side. The sky was then roughly selected using the *Rectangular Marquee* tool. Next, the *Move* tool was selected and the sky was physically dragged to the mountain picture. Elements automatically places the selection in its own layer above the original layer. This layer was renamed sky.

Still using the *Move* tool, the sky was roughly centred, but was not yet quite the correct size. It is important to note that resolution of both shots should ideally be the same or similar. If one shot has a much lower resolution than the other, the mismatch will be obvious.

3 On the original layer I used the *Rectangular Marquee* tool to select as much sky as possible without including any mountains.

Shoot a selection of different skies and build up a library to draw on when you need to replace one sky with another.

4 The *Magic Wand* tool was then used to add any remaining bits of sky not already selected. Hold down the Shift key to add further to the selection. To remove parts from a selection, hold down the Alt key before clicking with the *Magic Wand* tool. By changing the *Tolerance* setting, found in the *Options Bar*, you can specify the sensitivity of the *Magic Wand*. A *Tolerance* of 30 is good.

Zooming in helps to fine-tune the selection. For small areas within the sky that are still not selected, try using the *Lasso* tool again holding down the Alt key. If you make a mistake don't panic! You can go to the *Undo History* palette and step back to recover – keep going back one step until the problem disappears. This powerful feature has saved my bacon on many occasions!

5 Feather the selection to soften the edges. It helps to select any rogue pixels that were too small to pick up during the selection process. Use a *Feather* radius of 4 – too much and the selection edges start to lose their original shape.

Next, the grey sky was cleared and the selection was cancelled. The blue sky layer was then activated and dragged below the original mountain layer. This layer change allowed the sky to go behind the mountains.

6 As the sky was still too small, I used the *Scale* tool to change the size by dragging the corner handles, with the Shift key held down to keep it in proportion. The middle handles were then used to fine-tune the size. To move the sky, drag anywhere in the middle of the sky selection.

The original mountain layer was now activated to brighten the mountains slightly. Use *Levels* or the *Brightness/Contrast* controls for this. When I was satisfied with the image I flattened it to save disk space.

Simulating sunlight

2 First the general tone of the picture was brightened using *Levels*. This is a much more sophisticated means of tonal manipulation than *Brightness/Contrast*, so is well worth getting to know. The right-hand sliders were moved to the left. After change, the *Input* levels read 0/1.41/167. It's worth opening an image and playing around with the sliders so that you get an idea of how they interact.

Always at the mercy of the weather, the landscape photographer can't guarantee bright sunshine for a photo, even when the subject or composition demands it. It's fortunate, therefore, that Photoshop Elements gives us enough control to put some artificial sunshine into an image.

The *Levels* command can be used to enhance what light there already is in a picture and boost the colour and contrast, while other controls can add vivid colours that simulate the effects of brighter conditions.

1 This is a classic image shot in dull conditions. The photograph is slightly underexposed as there is no sun to boost the contrast.

As landscape photographers, we rely on the sun for light. We can use dull conditions to good effect, but some shots demand bright sunlight and clear, blue skies. Luckily, we can always put these in later on in software.

3 In order to enhance the green leaves I chose to select the yellow sunflowers and then invert the selection. With the yellow selected I swapped to the *Lasso* tool and manually selected the centres by hand. Hold down the shift key to add to the selection. Because the sky is pure white, there is no need to select it as its colour will not be affected.

Before | After

> **Tip**
> Select the brightness values you want to adjust (middle tones, dark areas, or light areas). Drag the Amount slider to set the intensity of the change. Click a thumbnail preview to make your image match it.

1. Select area of image to adjust.   3. Use buttons below to adjust your image.

○ Midtones
○ Shadows   Increase Red   Increase Green   Increase Blue   Lighten
○ Highlights
○ Saturation

2. Adjust Color Intensity.
Amount: Decrease Red   Decrease Green   Decrease Blue   Darken

4 I now chose *Color Variations* in the *Enhance* menu. The cold leaves need warming up, so I increased green, decreased blue and increased red. The *Decrease Blue* box increases the yellow by removing blue. Choose the midtone areas for general colour changes and a central setting for the *Adjust Colour Intensity* slider.

> **TIP**
> When making tonal changes, try using an adjustment layer. This allows you to return at any time and alter your settings; necessary if you change your mind later on in the process.

5 I decided to create a sun-like appearance to this shot by highlighting the four dominant sunflowers in the foreground. These will be brightened and the background darkened. First, I selected the middle of the sunflowers and brightened them using *Levels*. I then chose to adjust each flower individually. For a small area such as this it can be easier to use the *Contrast/Brightness* tool instead. Use the *Dodge* and *Burn* tools to manipulate even smaller areas.

```
                    Color Picker
Select foreground color:                    ( OK )
                                            ( Cancel )
                                            ( Help )

                                    ○ H: 208 °
                                    ○ S: 97 %
                                    ○ B: 88 %
                                    ○ R: 6
                                    ○ G: 122
                                    ○ B: 224
□ Only Web Colors                   # 067AE0
```

6 The sky now needed some colour, so a blue gradation was used. This is similar to using a graduated colour filter on your camera lens, but you have much more control over the exact colour. The rectangular *Marquee* tool was used and feathered by 15 pixels so that the transition at the bottom wouldn't be hard, jagged and obvious.

A blue colour was chosen from the colour picker. Go to the *Set Foreground Color* square on the main menu and double-click it – a dialog box will appear allowing you to choose a colour.

7 The background sunflowers are now selected so that they could be darkened to add to the sun and shadow effect. Carefully go around the edges of the main sunflowers until all the background ones are selected, using the *Lasso* tool. I usually do a rough selection first and then add to it using the shift key, or delete areas using the Alt key. This allows you to quickly build up an accurate selection. After feathering, *Levels* was used to darken the flowers.

8 The selection was then inverted to brighten the foreground further. When the selection was inverted, I had to deselect the sky area by using the *Lasso* tool while holding down the Alt key. I finally finished off by lightly brushing the leaves with the *Dodge* tool, using a soft brush and an *Exposure* of 10% to add speckled highlights to the leaves.

Rays of light

In the original shot I used the shapes of the clouds to create a natural-looking stormy dark cloud, from which the rays of light emerge. Simply select the shape, feather it and darken it using the Levels dialog box. I then reversed the selection (Select > Inverse) and used the Dodge tool to brighten the other side of the clouds to create a sun-behind-clouds effect.

H ere is another clever trick that adds extra character to a scene. Spectacular storm conditions can be caught on camera, but it takes luck, technique and patience. When you're running short on one of these, Photoshop Elements can inject some additional drama to the image by adding an artificial lighting effect. While this might seem inappropriate to a 'natural' subject like a landscape, the results can be very effective.

TIP Try looking for a shot that naturally allows for a stormy effect. If you can't find one, then try shooting a stormy sky and dropping it into the scene.

1 Use the *Polygonal Lasso* tool to create a nice straight line. Start the line at a point just inside the stormy cloud from which all the rays emanate, and go to the edge and bring the line back to a small point. It is worth saving each shaft of light as a separate selection so that they can be individually brightened to add a variety of textures to the shot. I feathered the selection by 55 pixels to give a soft edge.

2 With the selection still active, choose *Layer > New Adjustment layer > Levels* and move the midtone slider to the right to create the ray. Using adjustment layers, you can come back and fine-tune the brightness of each ray later to achieve the correct balance.

By the careful use of selecting, dull and lifeless shots can be given a new lease of life – some extra va-va-voom!

Now create more rays of light, using the same technique of soft-edged selections and *Levels* adjustment layers. When you get to the *Levels* palette, use different settings for different rays. This gives the rays different strengths, lending the image a more realistic feeling of depth.

3

4 Here, I created a shorter ray so I could make the town light up. I also selected the grass just in front of the town, and feathered and brightened it to make it look as if the end of the shaft of light was beginning to spill over. I darkened the foreground to add a sense of depth to the shot. Finally I used the *Burn* tool to darken the natural line of trees.

5 As a finishing touch, I used the *Clone Stamp* to remove one or two intrusive bright houses in the foreground area that had already been darkened.

FACT FILE

Achieving balance

Using a *Levels* adjustment layer after each selection is made enables you to go back and alter the brightness at any time if you change your mind. This is a great tool to master – every layer can be adjusted in this way. Choose *Layer > New Adjustment Layer > Levels*. (This allowed me to fine-tune the brightness of each ray to achieve the correct balance.) Use the *Eraser* tool to knock back part of the adjustment layer if it needs small local adjustments to the brightness. Simply go over the area softly, using a low *Opacity* setting. Remember to activate the adjustment layer by clicking on it before using the *Eraser* tool.

Filters and artistic effects

1 There are several types of filters that can produce a grainy effect. Choose strong, bold images with simple detail and texture for this treatment.

2 The *Grain* filter adds random pixels to give the effect of high-speed film. I chose an *Amount* of 60%, *Uniform Distribution* and checked the *Monochromatic* box, which applies the filter using the colour present in the image to achieve a purer colour.

Photoshop Elements comes with a large selection of filters for adding special effects to your images. As with traditional camera filters, it is possible to get carried away with all these effects. Many people think that a filter will rescue a bad photo – it more than likely won't, I'm afraid, but some filters can be used to add interesting effects. Used with care and intelligence, filters can help you produce works of art suitable for framing and hanging.

Try to experiment with different filter mixes and remember that by using the *Opacity* slider, blend modes and layers you have a vast combination of different effects available. Third-party companies also produce filter plug-ins, which can be installed into the Photoshop Elements plug-ins folder. Kai's Power Tools from Procreate is a good plug-in to buy once you've become bored of the Adobe filters.

3 It is sometimes better to add extra colour saturation and contrast before using the *Grain* filter, as these adjustments are not always so effective when the filter has already been applied.

In this example I used the *Diffuse Glow* filter with the following settings: *Graininess* 6, *Glow Amount* 10 and *Clear Amount* of 15. This gives a lovely soft-focus effect where the bright areas are deliberately overexposed.

1 The *Clouds* filter, found in the *Renders* section of the *Filter* menu, only creates one effect: random clouds. It works well to create a cloudy background, or – with the *Opacity* faded – a foggy foreground. Here, combined with the *Difference* blend mode, it creates a strange, otherworldly effect.

The original shot is an ideal image for having some filter effects applied to it. Strong colour and bold subjects such as these usually work well with filters.

5 Here the *Grain* filter was used with a setting of 48 *Intensity*, 60 *Contrast* and with the type set to *Speckle*. I then merged the *Speckle Grain* layer with the *Find Edges* layer and used a *Hard Light* blend mode. This has produced a nice drawing-like effect without destroying too much of the detail.

2 *Bas Relief* produces a similar effect to sandwiching a negative and positive film together. It works best when used with another layer and a non-*Normal* blend mode.

4 An interesting image, where the *Bas Relief* layer was merged with the *Clouds Difference* layer – the blend mode used was *Linear Light*.

3 The *Find Edges* filter creates fine lines at borders of contrast.

Filters and artistic effects

2 I then returned to the original layer and brightened it before positioning it as the top layer and using the *Hue* blend mode.

1 I used three images for this shot. The original layer was copied and given extra colour saturation and contrast. It was placed as the middle layer and the *Multiply* blend mode was applied.

Here I used *Find Edges* on a copy of the background layer, desaturating the colour then increasing *Brightness/Contrast*. The *Multiply* blend mode gives it a drawn look (left). Add another copy layer and boost the *Saturation* for this effect (right).

3 Finally, I made a further copy of this layer and used the *Glowing Edges* filter and put this as the bottom layer.

Black-and-white

here are several ways to create a black-and-white image. You could just shoot your images in greyscale, but I don't recommend this route. All digital cameras record more detail and information in colour than in black and white, which can give a higher-quality image when printed. Printing in greyscale can create posterized effects, in which the transition from one tone to the next is not smooth and continuous but stepped. Finally, you will have to go back and reshoot if you later decide you would prefer the image in colour.

Moreover, without a colour original there are certain image manipulations that you cannot do, such as combining a colour and greyscale image to form a tinted image. You will also need an RGB image to create sepia-tones, duotones and other colour tints.

As a general rule, therefore, I always shoot in colour, then convert the image later. There are two methods of converting that I use:
▶ Convert a colour RGB image by using the *Enhance > Adjust Color > Remove Color* command. This converts the colours to greyscale values in equal amounts, but remains an RGB image. This is important, as it needs to remain in the RGB mode to add colour to it later on, if required.
▶ Use *Enhance > Adjust Color > Hue/Saturation* and reduce the *Saturation* slider to -100%.
Either works, but creating a black-and-white image with real tone and definition is more than just a matter of converting it from colour. Through some creative manipulation of *Levels* and contrast, you can create something worthy of a fine-art print.

1 The original image was a colour RGB shot converted to black and white using the *Remove Color* command. Before you do anything else, remember to create a new duplicate layer at this point!

2 The foreground was selected to give it more mood by increasing contrast. The selection was feathered by 35 pixels.

Create beautiful, striking and moody black-and-white images from your colour shots, which you can turn into sepia tone as well.

TIP When you have spent time making a complex selection, it is a good idea to save it. This will save you time if you need to use the mask again at a later date.

3 I then chose the *Selection Brush*, with a brush size of 83 pixels and set to *Mask* mode, to turn the selection into a red mask. The *Overlay* opacity was set to 60% so that I could see the image underneath. I used a hard

brush, with the background colour selected to paint the straight edges of the gravestones out of the mask (I feathered the selection later to soften it). I then slowly erased all the relevant areas that I didn't want to alter tonally.

4 It takes time and care to build up a good mask. It can help to invert the mask and take a look at it in reverse, so that you can easily see which parts you missed.

Once the mask is complete, you will need to revert to the *Selection* mode in order to do any further manipulation. This is found in the *Options Bar* above.

5 With the selection finished, I used the *Levels* command to increase contrast and darken the foreground slightly.

6 I now inverted the selection so that I could work on the sky. I removed the tree and wall in shadow from the sky selection, as I didn't want them to go any darker, then used *Levels* to darken the sky, but didn't increase the highlights too much.

Black-and-white

7 I next selected the top part of the sky and feathered the selection by 35 pixels. With the selection active, I opened the *Levels*

palette and moved the black and grey sliders further to the right to create really dark, dramatic skies.

8 To a lesser extent, the same was done for the bottom part of the sky. This helped to create a stormy cloud effect similar to the one you would get through burning in

the sky using your hands on a print in the darkroom. Again, the selection was feathered by 66 pixels for a really soft edge.

9 The front of the ruined church was selected and the selection feathered by 35 pixels. Again, the Levels palette was opened and the tones made darker and given more

contrast. This gives greater emphasis to the front of the church and adds further impact to the shot.

10 To rectify the dark wall in shadow on the church I activated the original layer, selected it, feathered it and copied it to a new layer. This layer contained only the church wall and was placed above the background copy layer and later merged. *Levels* was used to increase brightness and contrast in the final wall after lightening.

For this variation I used the *Smart Blur* filter, followed by *Underpainting*, followed by *Gaussian Blur*. I placed this layer above the original layer using the *Darken* blend mode.

11 I used the *Dodge* tool with a brush size of 75 pixels, selecting the midtones from the range with an *Exposure* of 42%. I then darkened the edges of the wall, which were a little too bright.

FACT FILE

Adding effects

You can leave the image there, or use some effects filters to get some more intriguing variations.

Copy the layer and apply the filter to the top layer. A traditional darkroom technique is to add a little soft focus to the image during the printing stage. This gives a lovely glow where the shadows bleed into the highlights. Use *Filter > Blur > Gaussian Blur* to create a similar effect in Elements. Create a duplicate layer first and apply the filter effect to this. I chose a strong blur of 50 pixels. This layer was then used with the *Pin Light* blend mode.

I added a further original layer for a new effect. I used the *Find Edges* filter on this and placed the layer at the bottom of the stack. The original layer was placed above it and given a *Linear Light* blend mode.

12 Part of the foreground was now selected and feathered. *Levels* was opened once again, and I moved the midtone slider to the right to make the selection darker.

13 The upper foreground was selected, feathered and brightened. I used the *Brightness/Contrast* tool, nudging up to give the effect of sunlight.

Sepia and duotones

M ost images that work in black-
and-white will also work well
when converted to sepia or another
coloured tint. Try using the colour to
add to the mood already present.
For example, a winter scene would
look odd if it were a warm colour, so
use the blue end of the spectrum.

The beauty of the computer is that no
unpleasant chemicals need to be used to tone
the prints, as in traditional photography. For
me, the main strength lies in the fine-tuning
that is now possible. Precise colour shifts can
be created with no wasted paper or chemistry.
You can also create multi-coloured tri/quad
tones. It has to be said that Adobe Photoshop
Elements' big brother, Adobe Photoshop, does
offer greater control because it has more tool
options to work with, but then it costs a lot
more, too.

1 The original image can be converted to
black-and-white by choosing to
desaturate the colours using *Enhance > Adjust
Color > Hue/Saturation*. Push the saturation
slider to the far left to remove all colour
information. If you are starting with a
greyscale image you must convert it to RGB
mode, so that colour can be added to the
image, using *Image > Mode > RGB*.

2 Because I was trying to create a
sepia colour tone I didn't want to get
rid of all of the colour in this example.
Instead, I chose to tick the *Colorize* button,
which automatically creates a colour tint to
the image. The colour of the tint depends
on the colour you have selected in the *Set
Foreground Color* box. Choose a brown for
a sepia effect and blue for a blue tint, etc.
You can always use the *Hue* slider to try
out different colour tints. The *Saturation*
slider can be used to increase or decrease
the colour's intensity. The *Lightness* slider,
however, should not be altered when
creating colour tones.

3 The top shot is the effect of using a
brown colour in the *Set Foreground*
colour box and selecting *Colorize*. The blue
tone is the result of setting a blue colour.

Adobe Elements allows you to create many variations of colour from one image. You can create some great effects that emulate complex split-toned black-and-white images.

Hue/Saturation

Edit: Master

Hue: -10

Saturation: +79

Lightness: 0

OK · Cancel · Help

Colorize · ☑ Preview

Brightness/Contrast

Brightness: +60

Contrast: +60

OK · Cancel · Help

☑ Preview

4 Next, I copied the sepia brown layer to create a radical colour manipulation. Firstly, I increased the *Brightness/Contrast* by 60%. I then increased the *Saturation* using the *Hue/Saturation* command and altered the *Hue* slightly. This high-contrast image could now be blended with other layers, with the white areas not significantly altering the colours in the layers below. The saturated brown colours, on the other hand, would interact to produce a true duotone, tritone or even quadtone effect.

 TIP Use the power of the colour controls, layers and blend modes to mix interesting colours for your simulated tone prints. Experimentation is the key to success, as always.

Layers — More ▸

Darken — Opacity: 100%

Look:

brightness14/con...

colourize blue

colourize sepia

Background

5 This layer was placed above the blue, sepia and original black-and-white layers. I used the *Darken* blend mode so that it would combine with the blue layer below. The blue layer was given a *Lighten* blend mode and the sepia layer below this was given a *Soft Light* blend mode. Experiment to find out which blend mode works best, as the different effects produced can vary enormously.

6 For example, this would be the effect produced if you did nothing more than change the blend mode of the top layer from *Darken* to *Hard Light*.

7 The effect of changing the blend mode to *Linear Burn* in the top layer.

8 Here, I used the *Layers* palette eye icons to switch off visibility for the sepia layer, then used *Layer > Merge Visible* to merge the background layer with the blue layer and the *Brightness/Contrast* layer at the top.

9 This example illustrates the effect of merging the original background layer with the sepia layer and the *Brightness/Contrast* layer at the top.

Creating 'painted' landscapes

Photocopy

Detail 5

Darkness 15

100%

1 First of all I copied the layer. Having selected the duplicate, I used the *Photocopy* filter, which can be found in the sketch submenu of the *Filter* menu. I altered the *Detail* to 5 and the *Darkness* to 15.

2 The filter creates a dark edge around most solid colours and can produce a nice sketch-like effect. It is similar to using a pen to draw a thin outline around the main detail.

For many newcomers to digital imaging, creating an image that looks like a painted work of art is just a matter of going straight to the *Artistic* section of the *Filters* menu and applying the effect. This approach will work well with the right photo, but you can get more subtle or interesting results by using other effects in conjunction with blend modes.

This is a fairly straightforward image where only one filter has been applied. Sometimes the simplest approach works best. I often find myself getting carried away with one filter after another. It can be good fun, but holding yourself back to one effect concentrates the mind.

Layers More

Soft Light Opacity: 100%

Lock:

photocopy

Layer 0

3 To finish, I blended the layer with the original using the *Soft Light* blend mode for a subtle effect. This blend mode keeps the shot from going too dark.

DIGITAL DARKROOM TECHNIQUES

The *Poster Edge* filter produces a lovely effect. It has a mezzotint etching feel to it, caused by the fine black lines and the texture it creates.

PAINTING AND BLENDING

Of course, there's nothing wrong with using the *Artistic* filters to create painterly effects – that's what they are there for, after all. You still get better results by applying them in layers and using blend modes to mix them.

1 This simple shot of a Spanish golf course stands up to a whole variety of treatments. Again, I used single filters and combined them with blend modes when I wished to obtain a particular effect.

2 *Filter > Artistic > Paint Daubs*. This filter creates an abstract painterly effect. I used a *Brush Size* of 23 and a *Sharpness* value of 40 and chose the *Simple* brush in this example.

TIP To check the effects of different filters, copy a small area of your image, and paste it into separate layers in a new document several times. Apply your chosen filters to each copy in turn and then compare them to see which works best.

3 This is *Paint Daubs* again, but here I used the *Darken* blend mode on the filtered layer and blended it with the original background copy image to produce a more subtle painterly effect.

Faking infra-red film

1 First of all, I used the *Replace Color* command. I selected all the blue sky using the *+ Eyedropper* tool and dragged the fuzziness slider so that no foreground was selected. I then dragged the lightness slider to -100. This darkened the sky considerably and removed most of the colour.

Traditional photographers have created interesting effects using a combination of infra-red films and filters. Using infra-red film doesn't make too many technical demands on the experienced darkroom worker, but its requirements in terms of focusing, exposure and development can make it tricky. Photoshop Elements has a somewhat laborious but worthwhile method of creating a pseudo black-and-white infra-red image.

2 I then went into *Hue/Saturation* and chose the yellow colour and pushed the *Lightness* slider to +100. The same was then done for the green colour. This action brightened the green/yellow colours. I then used the *Enhance > Adjust Color > Remove Color* command to remove the colour from the image. At this point I also created a copy layer so that any manipulations made to it could be combined with the original layer to create the final image.

You can achieve an effect similar to colour infra-red photography by making careful selections with the magic wand tool, then applying excessive *Hue* adjustments using the *Hue/Saturation* control.

5 Using the original layer again, I created a selection for the foreground, but did not include the castle in the selection because it had lost detail. I feathered the selection by 25 pixels for a soft edge and then chose *Edit> Clear* to remove the dark foreground.

3 Now comes the weird bit. On the new copy layer, I went into *Levels* and chose the *Green* channel. Here I pushed the highlight slider up to 188, the grey slider up to 181 and the black slider to 7. This has brightened and boosted the contrast in the greens. It may look awful, but remember the final image will become black-and-white.

4 I then used the *Enhance > Adjust Color > Remove Color* command to get rid of the now-awful green colour. This has given a good infrared-style foliage, but the sky has gone too dark and contrasty.

6 This shows the original sky layer combined with the new foreground from the second layer. I thought the foreground was a little too bright, so used the *Levels* command to darken it slightly. The process might seem a little complicated, but you can't deny that it has produced an interesting image.

Making panoramas

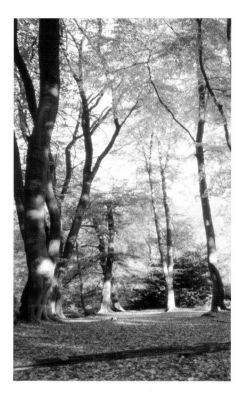

1 The four images I took for this scene were shot with the aid of a tripod and a spirit level. If a job's worth doing it's worth doing well, and *Photomerge* works better when you put in the groundwork first. I have found that it works best of all if you open each image up on the desktop first. This also allows you to check that all the images are present. The software automatically merges any images opened on the desktop when you select *File > Create > Photomerge*.

Adobe Elements has a great feature entitled *Photomerge* that allows you to easily create photographic panoramas. To do this, you need to have a selection of shots suitable for making a panorama. Using the wide setting of your lens, take between four and eight portrait shots of your chosen subject. Remember to use the same focal setting for each shot, as changing the setting by zooming in will ruin the effect, and try to shoot from the same position. Using the same exposure for each shot helps to maintain consistency.

A tripod and spirit level will make taking shots for panoramas much easier. Obviously, the tripod keeps the shots nice and straight and allows more precise alignments than handholding the camera. The spirit level should be used before each shot to keep the camera angle consistent as you rotate the viewpoint.

You can shoot more frames if you want a wrap-around effect, and you can also use the landscape format if you wish. However, the process tends to chop off top and bottom, meaning that too much image may be lost. Landscapes also suffer more from wide-angle distortion, so the merged shots may look a little strange.

The main trick is to make sure each picture overlaps the next by about 20%. This allows the software plenty of scope to produce a nice, soft, seamless transition from one shot to the next. Too much or not enough overlap can cause problems. This technique works well with any subject, whether landscape, cityscape or even an interior.

2 The *Browse* dialog box opens to confirm your selection. Choose the *Browse* option to add further images or to choose an entirely different set from scratch.

3 Click *OK* and the *Photomerge* software automatically merges the selected images to create a panorama.

4 At times *Photomerge* needs a little help, and the whole process becomes much harder. You may have to manually drag each image from the light box to the work area yourself, using the *Move* tool. You then have to judge by eye where each image overlaps. This is a lot more difficult than you might imagine, as what looks like a good overlap can end up with gaps in it after processing. Try clicking the *Snap To Image* box, as this helps the software to detect a good match when manually merging two or more images.

5 This is the final result. In some cases, you may find some areas of sky have irregular colour and density. Checking the *Advanced Blending* mode should minimize any exposure differences between shots, but does not always work. If not, I generally use the *Gradation* tool to put a colour grad over the problem.

A successful *Photomerge* should have little distortion to the images at the edges. Don't use a really wide wide-angle lens or the resulting distortion will not be easily rectifiable.

TIP There is a special panorama head available for tripods. This allows the process to be done very accurately, for truly professional results.

Montage: windmill at sunset

1 The original was quite a nice shot taken during the day, but due to nagging family members I couldn't hang about for the shot I really wanted – a sunset. I decided instead to create my own sunset. I quickly realized that the key to this would be a selection mask for the windmills.

By now it should be clear that the natural approach to landscape isn't always the most effective, and by making larger changes to the colours or tones, or even introducing new elements into the frame, you can create really exciting images. Now we're going to take this concept one step further, showing how you can composite multiple images to create a vista that looks as natural or unnatural as you want, but which has never actually existed.

2 The original shot taken with a moderate telephoto lens. I needed to find a suitable sea sunset. The windmills would go black, simulating a silhouette, so I wanted a strong yet simple sunset that was not too dark or the windmills would get lost in the background.

3 First I created a selection mask to turn the white windmills black, by creating a high-contrast image first. Create a new copy layer of the background. Choose *Brightness/Contrast* and boost both. This allows much sharper transitions in colour and density, which in turn allow for easier selections.

Sometimes a lot of work has to go into an image to make it look as though no work has gone into it at all. A thorough knowledge of selections is necessarry to create great-looking montages.

4 Use the *Magic Wand* and click on a black area. Most of the windmills' sails will be selected, but you can use the *Select Grow* and *Similar* commands to let the software hunt for pixels of a similar colour.

6 Switch back to *Mask* mode, and you can use a wide brush to quickly fill in areas that need to be masked.

8 Create a new layer. This is important, as you want to be able to move the layer to the top of the pile when finished. Fill the selection with black to simulate a silhouette. The sunset will be dropped in behind later. I slightly blurred the silhouette using *Gaussian Blur*. This is a standard technique to reduce the cardboard cut-out effect.

9 Now all that was needed was a sunset. I chose the top section of one I liked and blew it up to fit the document size. I was looking for a simple shot, as too many dark clouds would have interfered with the delicate sails of the windmills. This layer was placed below the silhouette.

5 Use the *Selection* brush found in the *Tools* menu. Invert the selection and select *Mask* from the *Mode* option on the top *Menu Bar*. The mask area shows up red (you can change this colour in *Preferences* if you wish) instead of the usual marching ants. Simply brush over areas that you want to add to the selection. You will find that this allows fine detail to be built surprisingly quickly. Click the mode back to *Selection* to check that you've got everything.

7 Remember the red areas in reality are non-selected areas, but because you inverted the selection you can paint in red. Just remember to invert the selection afterwards. The final mask should look like this when you have finished. Simply choose *Selection* when finished to return to the marching ants style selection.

Montage: sea

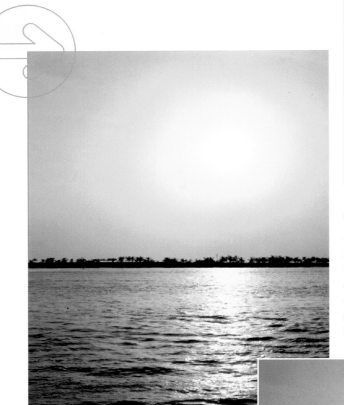

3 I then opened up a suitable sky to add to the sea, as the sun in the original was too overpowering for my taste. I resized to fit the width of the sea picture. Next, I dragged the sky over to the sea image using the mouse with the *Move* tool selected. This is a quick and easy method of moving layers from one document to another.

1 Initially I wanted to create a moonlit feeling, so I chose to make the orange Key West sunset blue. This was done using *Enhance > Adjust Color > Hue/Saturation*. I turned the sunset colour to blue by decreasing the *Hue* to -180 and increasing the *Saturation* to +100.

2 Next, I darkened the sea by moving the black slider to the right.

Levels

Channel: RGB

Input Levels: 27 1.00 255

OK
Cancel
Help
Auto

Output Levels: 0 255

Preview

4 I was looking for a feeling of loneliness on the open sea, so I removed the sky and trees on the horizon. I erased the old sky from the sea picture by selecting it with the *Rectangular Lasso* tool, then feathered the selection by 9 pixels to give a soft transition when layered with the new sky. I moved the sea layer to the top, so that I could move the sky up and down until I found the right position.

TIP If Elements slows down, use the *Edit > Purge* commands. These remove redundant data, such as *Undo History* steps from RAM. Check to ensure you are happy to lose them first.

Quite often, looking through your old images can spark the imagination into creating a new montage.

5 To make the sky more in keeping with a moonlit sea, I decided to make it bluer. I achieved this by desaturating the colour, by moving the *Saturation* slider to -100. I then went into the *Color Variation* menu and kept clicking the *Increase Blue* box and also clicked the *Increase Red* once.

6 I now opened the boat document to select and add the boat to the sea picture. I used several selection methods, including the *Magic Wand*, *Lasso* tool and *Selection Brush* tool to create the final complete selection.

7 As the boat was going to be in shadow, I created a new layer and filled it with black. Creating a new layer allowed me to drag it across to the sea document quite easily. It remains in its own layer when doing this, which is useful as I now needed to resize the boat using *Free Transform*.

8 The boat needed tidying up. I had to hand-draw some of the boat using the *Brush* tool with a small brush size. I also cleaned up the sails and post. In order to make the boat look more believable within the sea, I used the *Gaussian Blur* filter to reduce the sharpness slightly. This may sound odd, but images pasted into another document always look a little cut-out and obvious if this isn't done. A *Radius* of 1.5 was used.

9 Finally the moon was imported. It's a good idea to keep a stock of commonly used images, such as moons and skies, in a file for easy and quick access. The moon was resized using the *Free Transform* tool and placed above the reflections to follow the highlight patterns in the sea. I copied the moon layer and added a little *Gaussian Blur*. The moon also has a glow in real life, as it's so bright.

4 Showing your pictures

Having taken the time to shoot your landscape photos, and made the effort to manipulate them in the digital darkroom, it is only natural to want to show them to a wider audience. Whether this audience is family, friends or photographic peers, digital photography doesn't leave you short of ways to present your work. Prints can still be the most direct medium, but e-mail and the World Wide Web will allow you to share your photography with the world at large.

Perfect prints

Having gone to great lengths to take a picture, most photographers will see the output print as the final goal – something that can be framed and hung up on the wall in pride of place. Getting perfect prints can be a trying job at times. You need to set up the monitor and printer to give consistent results. Without this set-up you can end up wasting huge amounts of very expensive ink and paper.

PRINTER DPI

Inkjet printers work by spraying very small drops of cyan, magenta, yellow and black ink (CMYK) onto the paper surface. The idea is to create a printed image with the illusion of a continuous-tone photographic print. Each droplet is measured in picolitres; and modern printers can vary the size of these droplets in order to create better tonal separation. Most inkjet printers have a print resolution of 1440dpi or more, which is more than adequate for good-quality printing. Obviously, the higher the figure, the finer the printer resolution will be. For the ultimate in inkjet quality, some printers go as high as 5760dpi. This really only allows for finer tonal separation rather than finer detail.

The important thing to realize is that a printer's dpi resolution is different from the ppi resolution of an image on your computer screen. A printer needs to create dozens of very tiny 'dots' to fill the space of one pixel – hence the value of 1440dpi. Although a printer's output specifications are defined as 'dots per inch', it would be more accurate to think of them as 'droplets per inch'.

PPI V. DPI

The image captured by a digital camera is made up of pixels: tiny squares of colour information. The more pixels per square inch in an image, the finer the resolution and print detail will be. You can equate pixels per inch with dots per inch under normal working parameters. Adobe Photoshop Elements uses pixels per inch, while old-fashioned professional repro houses use dots per inch.

Film scanners scan at very high resolution, but the actual size of the film material is very small. A 35mm slide measuring 24 x 36mm will, for example, scan at up to 6000dpi. This figure will have to change, however, when you enlarge the image up to A4 size. An A4 image would be 210 x 297mm and, if left at 6000dpi would produce a very large file indeed – something like 5.5Gb!

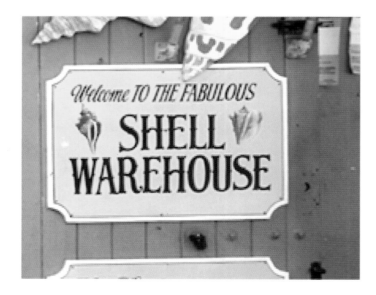

At 100ppi there aren't enough pixels to make this image work on the page. Look for tell-tale signs of pixelation around the curves of the letters and in the detail on the shells.

At 200ppi the resolution is high enough for an acceptable print, but not quite true photo- quality. At a distance everything should look fine, but close scrutiny will still reveal problems.

Understanding the difference between screen resolution and printed resolution is the key to getting perfect prints from your digital images.

WHAT RESOLUTION OR DPI / PPI DO YOU ACTUALLY NEED TO PRINT AT?

Basically this boils down to how the eye perceives detail. The human eye can only resolve detail up to certain limits. For most printed purposes, where the image is viewed at 8-12 inches, this equates to an image of 300 to 400dpi/ppi. Such a resolution is ideal for our brain to be able to visualize the image as a continuous tone.

INK AND PAPER

Until you have enough confidence to choose inks from other suppliers, I would advise using the manufacturer's inks. Some companies such as Lyson produce high-quality inks that rival manufacturers' own inks, but in general it is advisable to use only Epson or Canon inks in their respective printers. Beware cheap inks! They often clog up the nozzles and produce inferior print quality. In the long run they cost more because they are so unreliable.

Papers, on the other hand, offer much more choice. I rarely use manufacturers' own-brand paper and prefer ICI Olmec paper. I use a glossy heavyweight 260g paper, which yields good blacks and good colours. It prints extremely well on Epson and Canon printers. Matt photo papers are also good and may be perfect for framing as there is less glare from reflections compared to glossy prints. There are many other brands out there that offer a good compromise between price and quality. You may like to try out several brands to find the one that suits you. Papers don't cause problems with printers in most cases, but take care if using non-inkjet papers and do careful tests first as these could jam inside the printer.

Different papers will give surprisingly different results from the same file printed on the same printer. I suggest sticking to one brand to maintain consistency in printing, though it is possible to create and save custom colour print profiles using the printer software.

You can then simply choose the profile from the *Custom* menu bar. One paper, for example, may print with too much magenta, so you can dial in less magenta and save the profile instead of manually correcting the colour.

CHOOSING THE RIGHT PRINTER

If your ultimate goal is to produce top-quality landscape prints you will need a good printer or all your hard work will be for nothing. Look out for a printer that offers photorealistic printing and check print samples carefully. Try to get a printer with at least six colour inks. The extra light cyan/magenta inks make much smoother tones in the print quality. You can also get printers with light black ink for even greater tonal control. Make sure you buy a printer with separate ink cartridges for each colour (i.e. six or seven separate ink cartridges). All-in-one ink cartridges waste huge amounts of ink. When one colour has finished all the others have to be thrown away.

At 300dpi there are enough pixels to produce photo-quality output. Pushing the image resolution past this point will rarely have any benefit when the shot is printed out.

The screen is far more forgiving when it comes to image resolution. If viewed at actual size, a 72ppi image will appear to be photo quality. It is only when the image is printed out that the pixels that make up the shot become obvious. For Web or e-mail use, 72ppi is perfectly adequate.

Perfect prints

1 Picture quality depends on the resolution of your image. Try to use 300dpi as your standard document resolution. You also need to make the photo the correct size for the paper. If you have enough resolution for a full-size A4 print, make sure there is room for a small border around the edge of the paper.

3 Choose *File > Print Preview*. This is useful, as you will automatically see if you've chosen the wrong orientation – this can save wasted paper and ink in the long run.

5 When you are happy with the size and layout select *File > Print*. Before you press the button, it is well worth doing a final check on the most important settings.

2 Choose *File > Page Setup* from the main *Menu Bar*. Select landscape or portrait orientation and your chosen print size. You can also choose scale or borderless printing on newer printers.

4 Now would be a good time to put some paper in the printer! Remember to put the paper in the right way up. Gloss is easy, but some single-sided matt papers are difficult to judge, especially in artificial light at night. The whiter side is the one to print on. Mark the envelope or packaging so you know which is the front, for future printing.

6 The printer dialog box will open. You can use the basic auto-print, photo enhance or custom. Choose a paper type: if you don't have an exact match use the closest one on the list. Use *Speed* for quick, unimportant work and *Quality* for best work. Click on *Custom* and then *Advanced* to create your own profiles. Use the colour controls in the *Color Management* section and play around with the settings until you get a perfect print. This may take a while! You can then save the setting for future use. Finally, hit the *Print* button.

TIP Try to print during the day so that you can use window light to check the colours are true to life. Looking at a print under artificial tungsten lights will make it appear warmer than it is. Under fluorescent or low-energy bulbs it may even look green.

SHOWING YOUR PICTURES

In Photoshop proper, standard RGB (Red, Green, Blue) images should be converted to CMYK (Cyan, Magenta, Yellow, Black) prior to printing. Elements takes care of this for you automatically.

Callibrating your display is a chore, but one that makes a difference when it comes to printing and sharing your shots. You need accurate colour across every device in the chain to get superb prints.

1 Choose *Custom* in your printer dialog box. Then choose advanced.

2 Choose *Color Controls* in *Color Management*.

3 You now need to decide if the print is too dark or too light, and what colour to add or subtract. Density, contrast and saturation are straightforward. Working out a colour cast is not always easy, but trial and error should get you there in the end. For quality results, uncheck *High Speed* and check *Finest Detail*. Choose a paper and print quality setting for the job in hand.

4 Once happy with the colour and density, you can save the setting. Do as many tests as you like for different papers.

POOR COLOUR QUALITY

Bad colour casts or the wrong density can be a problem. If they are, then you will have to calibrate your monitor or your printer. This simply means matching up the print to the monitor, or vice versa, for reliable printouts. Your monitor may be too dark or too green, for example, so any colour corrections you do will be wrong in the first place. You have two options. Firstly, use a custom printer profile to correct the problem at the print stage; or, secondly, calibrate your monitor. Often you may need to do both. Calibrate the monitor and then the printer.

MONITOR CALIBRATION

The monitor can give inaccurate colours and density. The room lighting can also affect the monitor's colours, so I advise you to use a black-card cover 6-8 inches around the monitor to stop reflections. This is easy to make and need not be attached permanently. Don't allow strong sunlight to reflect off the monitor and cause glare.

You can use Adobe Gamma correction supplied with Adobe Photoshop Elements. It may already be installed on your computer, so check your control panels first. The calibration process is fairly straightforward, but you can use a wizard if necessary. A tip is to squint when trying to fade the grey boxes together – it's much easier. You should also try to do it in a darkened room for greater accuracy.

PRINT CALIBRATION

The following example is for an Epson printer, but Canon and other manufacturers' printer calibration methods will follow a similar process.

FACT FILE

TIP Reducing colours in the printer colour correction will use less ink than increasing a colour.

Understanding colour corrections

Print is	Colour variations in Elements	Printer colour correction
TOO CYAN	Increase red	Reduce cyan or increase magenta + yellow
TOO YELLOW	Increase blue	Reduce yellow or increase cyan + magenta
TOO MAGENTA	Increase green	Reduce magenta or increase cyan + yellow
TOO GREEN	Increase magenta	Increase magenta or reduce cyan + yellow
TOO BLUE	Increase yellow	Increase yellow or reduce cyan + magenta
TOO RED	Increase cyan	Increase cyan or reduce magenta + yellow

Creative borders

Adding a border around your image helps to provide the finishing touch to your work. Although Adobe Photoshop Elements has several borders and frames to choose from in the *Effects > Frames* menu, they will soon become monotonous to use.

1 For this shot, I used a pre-drawn black mask made using black ink on paper. The image was scanned in using a flatbed scanner and imported into the sunset shot. With the black mask on a separate layer, choose *Screen* from the blending mode pull-down list. The blending modes are very powerful and can produce really cool effects.

2 I used the *Eraser* tool and the *Maple Leaf* brush to create this interesting border design. Keep altering the brush size for varied leaf sizes.

Photoshop Elements offers a number of border effects in the *Effects > Frames* menu. Some are useful and some are a little over the top. The *Layer Styles* palette is another great source of creative border effects.

Why not try to make your own border? It isn't that hard and you will be the proud owner of your own unique border style.

Although you can buy some great plug-in filters for borders from companies like Extensis, it is more fun and more rewarding to create your own, not to mention a lot cheaper! There are several different ways to make them.

TIP Hundreds of everyday objects can be employed as frames if you scan them. Try using a black cloth over any 3D objects you scan to stop stray light and flare wrecking the shot.

TIP Use the *Free Transform* tool to reshape the black mask border to any shape you want.

FLATBED SCANNING

If you have a flatbed scanner you can draw your own border on paper. This opens up many different permutations of paper and media that you can use. Try watercolour paper and wet paints and scan the results in. You could even scan a real picture frame or any other 3D object using a flatbed scanner. The only limits are your imagination!

CAMERA COPY

You can also use a camera to copy the artwork and input this file onto your computer.

BRUSHED BORDERS

This is perhaps the easiest route to take. Start by creating a new layer, filling it with white and placing it underneath the image. Now resize the canvas so that it is several inches larger all around. You can now use the Impressionist brush (click and hold on the *Brush* icon in the toolbar) to paint a border underneath or on the actual image. You can also use the eraser brush to remove image information rather than adding to it with the paint brush.

TIP To fill a layer with solid colour, double-click the *Set Foreground Color* box in the *Toolbar*. Choose a colour from the *Color Picker*, then choose *Edit > Fill* and click *OK*.

3 A simpler brush design, produced by a soft brush being used to remove parts of the image for a subtle, 'sponged' effect.

4 I ended up erasing the entire border three times – the *Opacity* was gradually increased each time I had finished going round.

5 A simpler and cleaner edge effect created by going around once at maximum 100% *Opacity*.

Greetings card

Creating a greetings card will give your work a professional and slick appearance. You can use these cards to impress your friends – or even to send to an important client, who might be flattered by a bespoke and unusual gift. Once you have made the design template you can reuse it time after time.

1 The first thing you need to do is find a suitable photograph that reflects what you are trying to portray. Here, I've chosen a moody winter shot. You will need to keep the original photo open and create a new document for the card itself.

2 The next hurdle is to decide what size you want the card to be. Here I've chosen a panoramic format, so the card's dimensions will have to fit the photo. I've decided that I will print onto an A4 sheet of paper, so the initial size is 8.3 x 11.7 inches. Use the *Image Size* dialog box to create this size. Choose white as the background colour and a resolution of 300ppi to maintain good-quality printing. You are now ready to fill the card with your background colour, which should be sympathetic to your photo.

TIP In many instances you can resize the image before pasting it into a new document, then make any minor changes of scale using the *Transform > Scale* tool.

3 The background colour of the card will be a blue colour to echo the cool colours of winter in the original. With the original winter image still open on the screen, I used the *Eyedropper* tool to select a blue to maintain a link between the photograph and the background colours. The blue colour should now appear in the *Set Foreground Color* square on the left-hand-side tool menu. I then clicked back onto the new A4 page and then chose *Edit > Fill* to apply the colour to the entire page. This will now become your background page with the photo in a layer on top of it.

Creating your own greetings cards is a simple and easy way to show off your work to friends and family.

4 It is now time to paste the winter image into the new A4 page that has been created. Check that the image resolution is the same for the photo and the document. If not, use the *Image > Resize > Image Size* to correct the resolution. Select all and use the *Move* tool to manually drag the image across to the A4 card page. It's easier if you have both windows open and next to each other when performing this. In this case, the photo was much larger than the A4 page was – don't panic! Use *Edit > Transform > Scale* to resize the image. Simply drag the corner handlebar with the mouse. To maintain a proportional size, hold down the shift key whilst resizing. Alternatively, use the percentage values in the *Menu Bar* at the top. Click the middle icon and fill in a percentage in one of the boxes. Make sure there is a border of equal width on both sides and on the bottom. If necessary, select the *Move* tool and use the arrows on the keyboard for very precise incremental movements.

5 For a more professional look, a thin white border was added around the image. Use *Select > All* and then *Edit > Stroke* and a dialog box will appear. Enter 3 in the *Width* box for a 3-pixel-wide border. Next, double-click the colour box to make the colour picker appear and choose a suitable colour, in this case white. Click *OK* and a white border will appear around the image. You could at this stage add a bevel edge or other effect from the *Layer Style* menu.

6 Next, some type was added to the image. The *Type* tool is a very powerful vector tool within the Adobe Photoshop Elements software that allows for the creation of some sophisticated styles. Because of this you don't need to buy an expensive page-layout package.

For the font I chose Papyrus Regular with a size of 45. Before typing, select a colour from the colour picker in the *Options Bar*, or double-click the *Set Foreground Color* icon. You can change the colour at any time by selecting the type first. Click on the *Type* tool and a new layer is automatically created – simply click in the area where you wish to begin writing. If the size is too big or too small, you can create a new font size by selecting the type with your mouse and typing in a new number. If you are familiar with typing in a word-editing package, these skills will come in handy when using the *Type* tool.

By floating the mouse cursor just to the side of the type the icon changes to a *Move* tool, allowing you to manually move the type by dragging it.

Greetings card

greeting card.psd @ 12.5% (B...

BACK OF CARD

MERRY CHRISTMAS

12.5%

greeting cardfront.psd @ 15% (solid colour, RGB)

BACK OF CARD

MERRY CHRISTMAS

14.96%   8.3 inches × 11.7 inches

8 The card was now a different size from the A4 paper. This meant I had to crop it, so that an exact-sized copy could be made to allow the inside text to be designed and placed accurately within a template. To find out the exact size of the bottom half, I created a new layer and then selected the bottom half of the card, again with the *Rectangular Marquee*, filling it with a different solid colour (green) while still on a new layer. This was then moved up until the two halves were back to back, clearly showing me where to crop the remaining white so that two equal halves were made for folding later. You can design the image to fit any shape. Keeping the two halves equal at the start will make this project easier.

7 To save on ink, the back of the card was made white. I created a new layer and selected the area above the red line with the *Rectangular Marquee* tool. I chose a white colour then used *Edit > Fill* to turn it white. This layer was placed above the blue background layer.

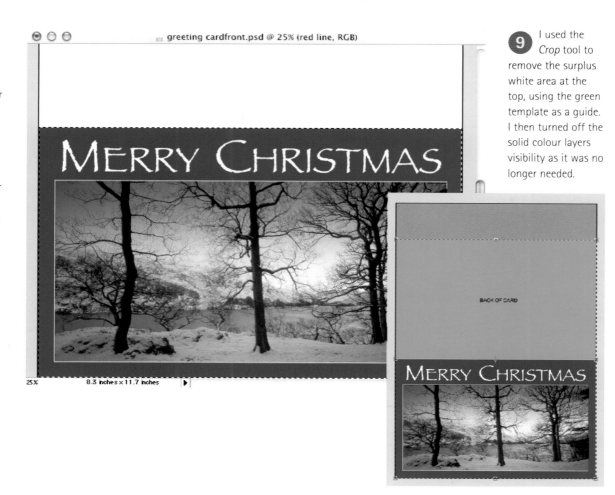

greeting cardfront.psd @ 25% (red line, RGB)

MERRY CHRISTMAS

25%   8.3 inches × 11.7 inches

9 I used the *Crop* tool to remove the surplus white area at the top, using the green template as a guide. I then turned off the solid colour layers visibility as it was no longer needed.

BACK OF CARD

MERRY CHRISTMAS

You can use the basic ideas and techniques in this step-by-step project to create other designs, such as a photographic letterhead for your stationery.

10 I opened the image size to make a note of the size and resolution, then created a new document using the same size and resolution. By keeping both documents open, I was able to select the solid green colour layer and drag it to the new document. This recreated the green template so that text could be correctly designed and accurately placed.

11 Next, create a new layer for the design located at the bottom of the card. Make a selection using the *Rectangular Marquee* tool to create a rectangle. Choose *Edit > Stroke* to create a blue border effect. I used a *Width* of 20 pixels and checked the *Inside* button in the *Location* box. The colour selected was blue, in keeping with the winter effect.

12 Finally, the *Spatter* filter was used to add texture. This is located in the *Brush Strokes* section. I chose a *Spray Radius* of 20 and a *Smoothness* of 2 for a coarse result.

TIP Try a mock-up card using a sheet of paper similar to the one you are going to print on and roughly draw how you want the design to look. This is a useful reference guide.

FACT FILE

For a different look
Add a little fun to the text box by using the *Liquify* filter to distort the shape of the box. For the 'one whisky too many' look you can distort the text as well, using the *Warp* tool!

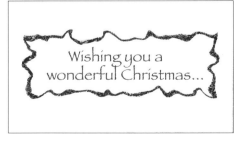

Greetings card

Calendar

CALENDAR BY TIM GARTSIDE 2004

1 I used a bold typeface, 'Impact', to allow me to make the text transparent later on, so that images would show through. Each line was created on a separate layer so that they could be moved independently. The 200pt font size was set manually to make the text fit the page, and I also used *Layer Styles* to create a bevel, adding shape and form to the text.

2 I used a photograph of some frozen glass beads as an alternative to the black background. Simply select the type, then go back to the blue bead layer and clear to reveal the photographs underneath. Use the *Layer Styles* to create the bevel effect again.

Some projects need to be split into manageable parts. I created this calendar in two sections – a front cover and an inside-page template. Both documents have been created to print out on an A4 sheet, with a width of 11.7 inches and a height of 8.3 inches. The resolution is 300 ppi.

3 Several photographs were opened and imported to the front-cover document, before resizing with the *Free Transform* tool. For this you should select pictures that are bright and vibrant or they may make the typeface difficult to read.

If you are intending to print many copies, then choose the background colour with care, as black or any other solid colour will use up a huge amount of ink. Use double-sided glossy or matt paper, and print one month on each side so that you only use half the paper.

Typeface heading
This group of typefaces shows how different *Layer Effects* can radically transform an ordinary black-on-white typeface.

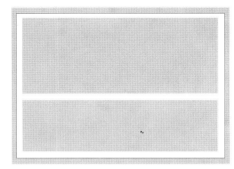

4 Finally, as a finishing touch I used a Wacom Art Pad to write the word 'Photography', which I placed in its own layer before resizing.

That's the outside taken care of. It's time to move on to the inside calendar page.

5 This is the basic design for the calendar-page template. I have split the page into an area for dates and an image. I will create two documents for the image and the dates and merge them together later.

Calendar

CREATING THE TEMPLATE DOCUMENT

Creating the grid and dates is a slow process, but one that is necessary for a professional look. You should be able to save the grid and text on separate layers so that amendments can be made for each month. This will be your master template, which you can duplicate for each month. Remember you can also make the calendar smaller by resizing it at the final stage. Use the *Save As* command to give it a new name. Remember to choose photos that reflect the particular month of the year.

1 A separate document for the date template was created measuring 11x 3 inches and 300dpi/ppi.

2 I used the grid so that aligning the dates would be easier. In *Edit > Preferences > Grid*, create a gridline every 1 inch. This creates a grid that is 11 squares long by three columns high.

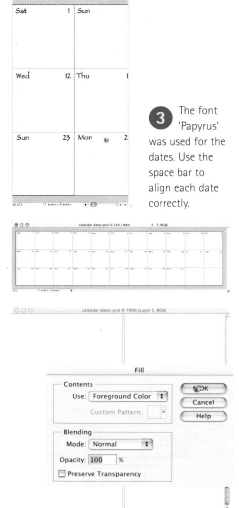

3 The font 'Papyrus' was used for the dates. Use the space bar to align each date correctly.

4 Create a new layer so that the box outline can be constructed. Use the *Rectangular Marquee* tool to create a line from top to bottom. Make it as thin as possible by zooming in to 700%, and then fill the line with black. Copy this layer and move it along to the next vertical grid line, then repeat the process and merge the thin line layers together.

5 Repeat the process to produce the horizontal lines, then flatten all the layers and import to the calendar-page template document.

6 The final page document needs to be a width of 11 inches by a height of 4.5 inches with a resolution of 300ppi. It should produce a nice panoramic effect in the final calendar design. A photograph of a sunset was opened and pasted into the photo template. It was then moved up and down until I was happy with the composition.

Creating a calendar is a big project but the end result has a powerful visual impact. Calendars can be a great way to present your work to others, or even sell your photography to potential clients.

7 The layers were then flattened and the image exported to the calendar-page template. With the photo and date as two separate layers above the white background layer, I now moved the two layers to create the final design.

SUNSET AT KEY WEST, FLORIDA

9 For an extra touch I created a *Stroke* line around each box, with a stroke *Width* of 3 to 6 pixels and a black colour.

8 I used the *Type* tool to add a subtitle in Helvetica Bold, 10pt and then created a new layer for the month. I chose a pale grey colour and a 200pt font size and wrote across the dates. I then adjusted the *Opacity* of the March type layer to 32% to make the type very faint, so you can read the text placed across it.

Preparing pictures for e-mail

1 Photoshop Elements will do most of the hard work for you at the press of a button. With the original image open, click on the *Attach to E-mail* button in the shortcuts bar or choose *File > Attach to E-mail*.

Attach to Email

Warning: The image you are sending may be too large for some recipients to download. Would you like Photoshop Elements to Auto Convert it to a smaller size or send the file as is?

(Auto Convert)   (Cancel)   (Send As Is)

2 If your image is too large, Elements will warn you and give you three options: *Cancel, Auto Convert* or *Send As Is*. If your recipient has broadband Internet access, you may be safe taking the last option. Otherwise, use *Auto Convert* and let Photoshop create a smaller, compressed version. Alternatively, click *Cancel* to make your own optimized image using the *Save for Web* option.

As almost everyone now has access to the Internet and e-mail, sending images to friends or family is now one of the easiest and most direct ways of sharing them. However, this usually requires a little preparation on your part. Not everyone has a fast broadband Internet connection, and large image files can clog up a slower Modem connection for longer than your image's recipient might care for. The trick to sharing images online is to learn how to shrink those file sizes down without adversely affecting image quality.

PREPARING AN IMAGE FOR E-MAIL.
If either you or your recipient has an older computer with a slow 28Kb modem, then choose a small file size of no more than 200Kb. For a 56Kb modem you can send file sizes of up to 1Mb, which is large enough for a good-sized print at 200 to 300dpi/ppi. You can send much larger files if you have the time. A broadband modem will allow you to send professional hi-res documents as long as the recipient has a broadband modem as well. I always keep low-res photos for e-mail in a specific folder, so that when I want to attach an image, I know where to find it.

3 If your image is OK in size, or you use the *Auto Convert* option, your e-mail application will open automatically and create a new message dialog box. Simply fill in the relevant details. The photograph should already be there as an attachment.

The strength of e-mail is its immediacy. One minute after you've sent your photo, Uncle Jim on the other side of the world can see what you have been up to.

SAVE FOR WEB

File	Edit	Image	Enhance	L
New...				⌘N
New from Clipboard				
Open...				⌘O
Browse...				⇧⌘O
Open Recent				▶
Create Photomerge...				
Close				⌘W
Close All				⌥⌘W
Save				⌘S
Save As...				⇧⌘S
Save for Web...				⌥⇧⌘S
Revert				
Attach to E-mail...				
Create Web Photo Gallery...				
Online Services...				
Place...				
Import				▶
Export				▶
Batch Processing...				

4 If you are preparing images for online use, or you want more control when attaching an e-mail, try the *Save for Web* command. This tool allows you to optimize your image for use on the Web, and will create the perfect balance between file size and image quality.

Image	Enhance	Lay
Duplicate Image...		
Rotate		▶
Transform		▶
Crop		
Resize	▶	Image Size...
Adjustments	▶	Canvas Size...
		Reveal All
Histogram...		Scale
Mode	▶	

5 If a dialog box appears saying that the file is too big for optimizing, then use the *Image > Resize > Image Size* command to reduce the size by a suitable amount.

6 A dialog appears, allowing you to change the size and resolution. For a reasonable file size, choose a size about 5 inches wide and a resolution of 100ppi. Now go back to *File > Save for Web*.

7 Another dialog box appears displaying your original photograph and the optimized version for the Web. You can see the file sizes underneath each version, while the optimized version also shows figures for quality and the time it would take for someone to download the image using a slow 28.8K modem connection.

TIP Click on *Progressive* to create a small low-res image that is displayed while the full image is downloading. Also, check that the *Constrain Proportions* box is ticked or the image may distort.

8 Here I have changed the settings from GIF to JPEG Medium with a quality of 60 using the *Custom* button.

9 The final quality setting of 30 has shrunk a file that was 551Kb in size to a mere 25.72Kb, with a minimal loss of quality.

10 To prevent overwriting the original file with a low-res version, you are prompted to save the file in a different place using a different name.

Pictures on the web

Adobe Photoshop Elements allows you to create your own web pages using various design templates. Some are good, some are fun and some, frankly, are for the kids. This is a great way to get some shots on the Web quickly and easily. Afterwards, you can upload the files to your web server or do further work in an application such as Macromedia Dreamweaver or Adobe GoLive. This is a powerful tool. Only a few years ago this work would have taken hours, or even days – now Adobe Elements can do it in minutes.

1 This shows the images that I want to turn into web pages. I've collected them all in one folder for ease of use. You can have as many as you like. For speed it is best to create small JPEGs first or the whole process gets quite slow. Use *Image Size* to reduce the file sizes if they are really big. I've just created one folder on the desktop and called it 'Sunsets'. At this point it is a good idea to create a second folder for the destination files. Create a new folder and call it 'Web Browser'. This is where you will save all the files you create. If you miss one file, the whole project fails to open, or parts of it are missing when viewing it in your web browser.

TIP On the Internet there is always the chance that someone will copy your work and use it illegally – so beware. In the *Options* drop-down menu there is a copyright option, allowing you to take measures that will prevent this from happening.

2 Go up to the *Menu Bar* and select *File > Create a Web Photo Gallery*

3 A dialog box opens with quite a lot of boxes to fill. Don't panic! Most of them just contain personal details to be displayed on your website, including your e-mail address and any contact information.

Antique Paper
Bears
Horizontal Dark
Horizontal Frame
Lace
Museum
Office
✓ Simple
Space
Spot Light
Table
Theater
Vacation
Vertical Frame
Wet

4 Click on the *Styles* drop-down menu to choose one of the web-page templates. You may want to try out several designs.

Putting your work on the Web allows potentially thousands of people to see it. It is a great marketing tool if you need one.

7 Click *OK* and your web page will be created, along with all of the necessary files, in the target folder. Double-click on it to open it in your browser. This is the antique-paper web page template.

Click on one of the thumbnails and a larger version appears with the same antique-paper design. Your website will now have a slick, professional feel to it, even if it took only ten minutes to produce.

5 Click on *Choose* and a new dialog box opens up to allow you to navigate to folders elsewhere on your computer. Select *Image Directory* – here I selected the 'Sunsets' file on my desktop. Place all folders on your desktop so you don't have too dig deep to find files. I then clicked on 'Sunsets' to open the file and make it active and clicked *Choose*.

6 Next I selected a destination location, which is where the folder 'Web Browser' comes into its own. Select 'Web Browser' from the menu and click *Choose*.

FACT FILE

Alternate template designs
Here, I've used a few more of the template designs. This one is called *Horizontal Dark*. In the *Options* menu for this design you can choose various different sizes for your pictures. The *Pixels* box lets you create your own custom size, if required. The higher the JPEG quality, the bigger the size, the longer each photo will take to open when you click on them while browsing on the Internet. Using your browser to test the speed offline will give a false impression, as there is no time lag when the photo is downloading from the ISP's server.

Glossary

aliasing The jagged appearance of diagonal lines in an image, caused by the square shape of pixels.

alpha channel A greyscale version of an image that can be used in conjunction with the other three colour channels for storing a mask or selection.

anti-aliasing The smoothing of jagged edges on diagonal lines created in an imaging program, by giving intermediate values to pixels between the steps.

aperture The opening behind the camera lens through which light passes on its way to the CCD.

application Software designed to make the computer perform a specific task. An image-editing program is an application, as is a word processor.

artifact/artefact A flaw in a digital image.

ASA American standard for film speed, roughly equivalent to the ISO rating.

aspect ratio The ratio of the height to the width of an image, screen or page.

autofocus A system used in traditional and digital cameras to ensure that the subject of a photo will be in focus at the moment the exposure is taken.

back-up A copy of a file kept for safety reasons, in case the original becomes damaged or lost. Make back-ups on a regular basis.

bit (binary digit) The smallest data unit of binary computing, being a single 1 or 0. Eight bits make up one byte. See also Byte.

bit-depth The number of bits of colour data for each pixel in a digital image. A photographic-quality image needs eight bits for each of the red, green and blue colour channels, making for a bit-depth of 24.

bitmap An image composed of a grid of pixels, each with their own colour and brightness values. When viewed at actual pixel size or less, the image resembles a continuous tone shot, like a photograph.

blend mode A setting in the Photoshop/Photoshop Elements layers palette, which controls how the pixels in one layer affect those in the layers below.

brightness The level of light intensity. One of the three dimensions of colour. See also hue and saturation

byte Eight bits — the basic data unit of desktop computing. See also Bit.

calibration The process of adjusting a device, such as a monitor, so that it works consistently with others, such as scanners and printers.

CCD (Charge-Coupled Device) A tiny photocell, made more sensitive by carrying an electrical charge before it is exposed, and used to turn light into an electronic signal. Used in densely packed arrays, CCDs are the recording medium in some scanners and most digital cameras.

CD (Compact Disc) Optical storage medium. As well as the read-only CD-ROM format, used by most computers to install applications, there are two recordable CD formats. On a CD-R (Compact Disc-Recordable), each area of the disc can only be written to once, although it's possible to keep adding data in different 'sessions'. On a CD-RW (Compact Disc-Rewritable) the data can be overwritten many times.

channel Part of an image as stored in the computer; similar to a layer. Commonly, a colour image will have a channel allocated to each primary colour (e.g. RGB) and sometimes one or more for a mask or other effects. See Alpha channel.

cloning In an image-editing program, the process of duplicating pixels from one part of an image to another.

CMOS (Complementary Metal-Oxide Semiconductor) An alternative sensor technology to the CCD, CMOS chips are used in ultra-high resolution cameras from Canon and Kodak.

CMS (Colour Management System) Software (and sometimes hardware) that ensures colour consistency between different devices, so that at all stages of image-editing, from input to output, the colour balance stays the same.

CMYK (Cyan, Magenta, Yellow, Key) The four process colours used for printing, including black (key).

compression Technique for reducing the amount of space that a file occupies, by using intelligent algorithms to reduce data.

continuous-tone image An image, such as a photograph, in which there is a smooth progression of tones between black and white.

contrast The range of tones across an image from bright highlights to dark shadows.

cropping The process of removing unwanted areas of an image, leaving behind only the most significant portion.

default The standard setting or action used by an application, unless deliberately changed by the user.

depth of field The distance in front of and behind the point of focus in a photograph in which the scene remains in acceptable sharp focus.

dialog An on-screen window in an application that is used to enter or adjust settings, or to complete a step-by-step procedure.

diffusion The scattering of light by a material, resulting in a softening of the light and of any shadows cast. Diffusion occurs in nature through mist and cloud-cover, and can also be simulated in professional lighting set-ups using diffusion sheets and soft-boxes.

digital A way of representing any form of information in numerical form as a number of distinct units. A digital image needs a very large number of units so that it appears as a continuous-tone image to the eye; when it is displayed these are in the form of pixels.

dithering A technique used to create an illusion of true-colour and continuous tone in situations where only a few colours are actually used. By arranging tiny dots of four or more colours into complex patterns, the printer or display produces an appearance of there being more than 16 million visible colours.

dMax (Maximum Density) The maximum density – that is, the darkest tone – that can be recorded by a device.

dMin (Minimum Density) The minimum density – that is, the brightest tone – that can be recorded by a device.

download Sending a data file from the computer to another device, such as a printer. More commonly, this has come to mean taking a file from the Internet or a remote server and copying it onto the desktop computer.

dpi (dots-per-inch) A measure of resolution in half-tone printing. See also PPI.

drag Moving an icon or a selected image across the screen, normally by moving the mouse while keeping its button pressed.

dynamic range The range of tones that an imaging device can distinguish, measured as the difference between its dMin and dMax. The dynamic range is affected by the sensitivity of the hardware and by the bit depth.

feathering The fading of the edge of a digital image or selection.

file format The method of writing and storing information (such as an image) in digital form.

fill-in flash A technique that uses the on-camera flash or an external flash in combination with natural or ambient light to reveal detail in the scene and reduce shadows.

filter (1) A thin sheet of transparent material placed over a camera lens to modify the quality of colour or light that reaches the film or sensor.

filter (2) A feature in an image-editing application that alters or transforms selected pixels for some kind of visual effect.

focal length The distance between the optical centre of a lens and its point of focus when the lens is focused on infinity.

focal range The distance over which a camera or lens is able to attain sharp focus on a subject (for example, 0.5m to infinity).

focus The optical state where the light rays converge on the film or CCD to produce the sharpest possible image.

fringe A usually-unwanted border effect to a selection, where the pixels combine some of the colours inside the selection and some from the background.

f-stop The calibration of the aperture size of a photographic lens.

GB (gigabyte) Approximately one thousand megabytes or one billion bytes (actually 1,073,741,824).

gradation The smooth blending of one tone or colour into another, or from transparent to coloured in a tint. A graduated lens filter, for instance, might be dark on one side, fading to clear at the other.

graphics tablet A flat rectangular board with electronic circuitry that is sensitive to the pressure of a stylus. Connected to a computer, it can be configured to represent the screen area and then be used for drawing.

greyscale An image made up of a sequential series of 256 grey tones, covering the entire gamut between black and white.

GUI (Graphic User Interface) On-screen controls that use icons and other graphic means to simplify using a computer or application.

handle Icons used in an imaging application to manipulate a picture element. They usually appear on-screen as small black squares.

histogram A map of the distribution of tones in an image in graph form. The horizontal axis runs from the darkest tones to the lightest, while the vertical axis shows the number of pixels in that range.

hot-shoe An accessory fitting found on most digital and film SLR cameras and some high-end compact models, normally used to control an external flash unit.

HSB (Hue, Saturation, Brightness) The three dimensions of colour, and the standard colour model used to adjust colour in many image-editing applications.

hue The pure colour defined by position on the colour spectrum; what is generally meant by 'colour' in lay terms. See also Brightness and Saturation.

image-editing program Software that makes it possible to enhance and alter a digital image.

interpolation A procedure used when resizing a bitmap image to maintain resolution. When the number of pixels is increased beyond the number of pixels existing in the image, interpolation creates new pixels to fill in the gaps by comparing the values of adjacent pixels.

ISO An international standard rating for film speed, with the film getting faster as the rating increases, producing a correct exposure with less light and/or a shorter exposure. However, higher speed film tends to produce more grain in the exposure, too.

JPEG (Joint Photographic Experts Group) Pronounced 'jay-peg', a system for compressing images, developed as an industry standard by the International Standards Organization. Compression ratios are typically between 10:1 and 20:1, but some data is permanantly lost. Higher levels of JPEG compression mean more loss, and therefore a lower quality image.

KB (Kilobyte) Approximately one thousand bytes (actually 1,024).

lasso A selection tool used to draw an outline around an area of an image for the purposes of selection.

layer One level of an image file, discrete from the rest, to which elements of an image can be moved or copied in order that they can be manipulated separately.

luminosity The brightness of a colour, independent of hue or saturation.

macro A mode offered by some lenses and cameras that enables the lens or camera to focus on an object in extreme close-up.

mask A greyscale template that hides part of an image. One of the most important tools in editing an image, it is used to limit changes to a particular area or protect part of an image from alteration.

MB (megabyte) Approximately one thousand kilobytes or one million bytes (actually 1,048,576).

megapixel A rating of resolution for a digital camera, directly related to the number of pixels forming or output by the CMOS or CCD sensor. The higher the megapixel rating, the higher the resolution of images created by the camera.

memory card The storage format used by most digital cameras, where images are saved to solid-state memory embedded in some form of small plastic housing. Common types include Compact Flash, SmartMedia, SD Memory Card and XD Memory Card.

menu In an application, an on-screen list of choices used to access features or change settings.

microdrive Miniature hard disk designed to fit in the memory-card slot of some digital cameras, and so increase the storage capacity.

midtone The parts of an image that are approximately average in tone, falling midway between the highlights and shadows.

mode One of a number of alternative operating conditions for a program. For instance, in an image-editing program, colour and greyscale are two possible modes.

noise Random pattern of small spots on a digital image that are generally unwanted, caused by rogue electrical signals.

paste Placing a copied image or digital element into an open file. In image-editing programs, this normally takes place in a new layer.

peripheral An additional hardware device connected to and operated by the computer, such as a scanner, modem or printer.

pixel (PICture ELement) The smallest unit of a digitized image — the square screen dots that make up a bitmapped picture. Each pixel carries a specific tone and colour.

plug-in Software produced by a third party and intended to supplement a program's existing features.

ppi (pixels-per-inch) A measure of resolution for a bitmapped image. See also DPI.

RAM (Random Access Memory) The working memory of a computer, to which the central processing unit (cpu) has direct, immediate access.

RAW A file format created by some high-end digital cameras, containing all the pixel information with no compression. Usually requires proprietary software supplied with the camera to view, adjust and convert the files.

re-sampling Changing the resolution of an image either by removing pixels (lowering resolution) or adding them by interpolation (increasing resolution).

resolution The level of detail in an image, measured in pixels (e.g. 300 ppi) or dots-per-inch (in a printed image, e.g. 1200 dpi).

RGB (Red, Green, Blue) The primary colours of the additive model, used in monitors and image-editing programs.

saturation The purity of a colour, going from the lightest tint to the deepest, most saturated tone. See also Hue and Brightness.

scanner Device that digitizes an image or real object into a bitmapped image. Flatbed scanners accept flat artwork as originals; slide scanners accept 35mm transparencies and negatives.

selection A part of the on-screen image that is chosen and defined by a border, in preparation for manipulation or movement.

shutter The mechanical device inside a conventional camera which controls the length of time during which the film is exposed to light. Many digital cameras don't have a shutter as such, but the term is still used as shorthand to describe the electronic mechanism that controls the length of exposure for the CCD.

shutter lag The time delay between pressing the shutter release on a digital camera and the exposure being made. This delay was a problem with early digital cameras

shutter speed The time the shutter (or electronic switch) leaves the CCD or film open to light during an exposure.

SLR (Single Lens Reflex) A camera that transmits the same image via a mirror to the film and viewfinder, ensuring that you see exactly what you are photographing.

spot meter A specialized light meter, or function of the camera light meter, that takes an exposure reading for a precise area of a scene. This is particularly useful for ensuring that vital parts of the scene are correctly exposed.

SuperCCD A CCD in which the pixels are oriented as diamonds. Processing the read-out of each line of pixels requires some interpolation, but gives a resolution higher than the pixel count.

telephoto A photographic lens with a long focal length that enables distant objects to be enlarged. The drawbacks include a limited depth of field and angle of view.

thumbnail Miniature on-screen representation of an image file.

TIFF (Tagged Image File Format) A file format for bitmapped images, which can use LZW compression (a compression technique that operates without losing any data). The most widely used standard for high-resolution digital images once they have been edited.

tool A program function specifically designed to produce a particular effect on-screen, activated by choosing an icon and using it as the cursor. In image-editing, many tools are the equivalents of traditional graphic ones, such as a paintbrush, pencil or airbrush.

toolbar An area of the screen used to provide immediate access to the most frequently used tools, settings and commands.

USM (Unsharp Mask) A sharpening technique achieved by combining a slightly blurred negative version of an image with its original positive.

vector graphic A computer image in which the elements are stored as mathematically defined lines, curves, fills and colours. Vector graphics can be scaled up or down at will without any effect on file size or resolution.

white balance A digital camera control used to balance exposure and colour settings for artificial lighting types with a different colour temperature than daylight.

zoom A camera lens with an adjustable focal length giving, in effect, a range of lenses in one. Drawbacks include a smaller maximum aperture and increased distortion over a prime lens (one with a fixed focal length).

Index

Acknowledgements

Thanks to Alan Buckingham for his help in forming the initial structure for this book, and for his advice during the early stages of its writing. Thanks, also, to the editorial and design teams at Ilex for their work on words and layout.

I would also like to thank Dominique Dallet, for encouragement and inspiration while I was shooting in Spain. Most of all, thanks to my wife, Yvonne Gartside, for her support, constructive criticism and creative input during every stage of this project.

Useful Addresses

Adobe (Photoshop, Illustrator)
www.adobe.com
Agfa www.agfa.com
Alien Skin (Photoshop Plug-ins)
www.alienskin.com
Apple Computer www.apple.com
Association of Photographers (UK)
www.the-aop.org
British Journal of Photography
www.bjphoto.co.uk
Corel (Photo-Paint, Draw, Linux)
www.corel.com
Digital camera information
www.photo.askey.net
Epson www.epson.co.uk www.epson.com
Extensis www.extensis.com
Formac www.formac.com
Fractal www.fractal.com
Fujifilm www.fujifilm.com
Hasselblad www.hasselblad.se
Hewlett-Packard www.hp.com
Iomega www.iomega.com
Kingston (memory) www.kingston.com
Kodak www.kodak.com
LaCie www.lacie.com
Lexmark www.lexmark.co.uk
Linotype www.linotype.org
Luminos (paper and processes)
www.luminos.com
Macromedia (Director)
www.macromedia.com

Microsoft www.microsoft.com
Minolta www.minolta.com
www.minoltausa.com
Nikon www.nikon.com
Nixvue www.nixvue.com
Olympus
www.olympus.co.uk
www.olympusamerica.com
Paintshop Pro www.jasc.com
Pantone www.pantone.com
Philips www.philips.com
Photographic information site
www.ephotozine.com
Photoshop tutorial sites
www.planetphotoshop.com
www.ultimate-photoshop.com
Polaroid www.polaroid.com
Qimage Pro
www.ddisoftware.com/qimage/
Ricoh www.ricoh-europe.com
Samsung www.samsung.com
Sanyo www.sanyo.co.jp
Shutterfly (Digital Prints via the web)
www.shutterfly.com
Sony www.sony.com
Sun Microsystems www.sun.com
Symantec www.symantec.com
Umax www.umax.com
Wacom (graphics tablets)
www.wacom.com